DIVINE DIRECTION

Saint Alex O. N. Asibey

DIVINE DIRECTION

1st Edition 2020
Copyright © Saint Alex Osei Nketia-Asibey, 2020

Author: Saint Alex Osei Nketia-Asibey
Text design: Schae Ind
Editor: Sheena Carnie
Cover design: Alexander Moolman

Printed in South Africa by Zeroplus

Copyright permission:
In terms of the Copyright Act 98 of 1978, no part of this book may be reproduced or transmitted in any form or by any means, electronic or mechanical, including photocopying, recording or by any information storage and retrieval system, without permission in writing from the publishers.

ISBN 978-0-620-88337-5

To order: aonasibey@gmail.com

This book is dedicated to Almighty God, my father; the Lord Jesus Christ, my saviour redeemer and mediator; the Holy Spirit, my comforter and intercessor; and Thearc Daniel Kingsley Arthur, my mentor and the founder of my church, Thearchical Domain.

ACKNOWLEDGEMENTS

I am greatly indebted to my wife, Lydia Asibey, and my children – Daniel, Solomon, Elizabeth, Linda and Emmanuel – who encouraged me to write this book and supported me throughout the work. My gratitude also goes to George Qua-Enoo who assisted with the manuscript, and to Abigail Tuffour and Jennifer Tuffour for typing it.

CONTENTS

THE CHURCH	7
WHO IS A CHRISTIAN?	11
WARNINGS TO TRUE CHRISTIANS	19
WARNINGS TO CHURCHGOERS	25
WHAT IS SIN?	31
REPENTANCE	35
BAPTISM	39
HOLINESS AND RIGHTEOUSNESS	47
WHERE CAN A PERSON GO AFTER DEATH	53
HOW CAN I GO TO HEAVEN?	59
FORNICATION	65
DEATH	69
WHO IS GOD?	75
WHO IS JESUS CHRIST?	79
WHO IS THE HOLY SPIRIT?	85
WHO IS SATAN?	91
WHO IS A SAINT?	97
ONCE SAVED NOT ALWAYS SAVED	101

LUST	105
ALCOHOL, SMOKING AND DANCING	111
HELL	117
AFFLICTION	123
WHAT IS FORGIVENESS?	127
CHRISTIAN PRAYER	133
CHRISTIAN FASTING	141
CHRISTIAN MARRIAGE	145
THE SOUL	153
WHY A TRUE CHRISTIAN SHOULD NOT WORRY	157
LOVE	161
THE BLOOD	167
BLESSING	171
MY EXPERIENCE WITH EVIL SPIRITS	177
MY CHURCH	183

INTRODUCTION

This book is meant for all mankind, especially for those who believe in God, and more especially for churchgoers who believe in God through Jesus Christ. I have used some of the most important verses in the Holy Bible to teach the greatest lesson that mankind should know – to become children of God who will go back to God after death. My prayer is that you will learn something you did not know before and will get a new perspective on some things you had taken for granted.

The history of mankind

Since the creation of the first man, Adam, only four people came into the world with the Holy Spirit and therefore were children of God, namely Adam, Eve, John the Baptist and Jesus Christ.

Adam and Eve were created in the image of God and with the breath of life became living souls with the Holy Spirit in them. John the Baptist received the Holy Spirit while he was in his mother's womb and therefore was born with the Holy Spirit, hence Jesus Christ stated in Matthew 11:11 *"Among them that are born of women, there hath not risen a greater than John the Baptist."* Jesus Christ was conceived by the Holy Spirit and born with the Holy Spirit.

God withdrew the Holy Spirit from Adam and Eve because of the sin they committed which was caused by Satan. God had warned them that if they ate from the tree of the knowledge of good and evil they would surely die, but they disobeyed God and ate the fruit and so they died. Their death was a spiritual death caused by losing the Holy Spirit. Since all men and women are descendants of Adam and Eve, all mankind has been conceived in sin and born in sin without the Holy Ghost. Thus the scripture in Psalm 51:5, *"In sin my mother conceived me."* Hence everybody born into the world commits sin.

Jesus Christ came into the world to conquer Satan and save us from sin so that whosoever believes in Him should not perish but have everlasting life, as we read in John 3:16. In John 3:3,5 Jesus Christ tells us the only way to become God's children again: *"Most assuredly, I say to you, unless one is born again, he cannot see the kingdom of God ... Most assuredly, I say to you, unless one is born of water and the Spirit, he cannot enter the kingdom of God."* The first birth is the physical birth of a child as a result of the union between husband and wife. The second birth is a spiritual birth, a supernatural birth, where God grants us the Holy Spirit and we become His children. It is only when a person becomes a child of God that they stop sinning, because the Holy Spirit in the person gives them power to overcome Satan and sin. This was the purpose of Jesus Christ coming into the world. A Christian is a child of God who does not commit sin; this is affirmed by the following verses from the Holy Bible:

- *"Whoever has been born of God does not sin, for His seed remains in him; and he cannot sin, because he has been born of God."* (1 John 3:9)

- *"Whoever abides in Him does not sin. Whoever sins has neither seen Him nor known Him."* (1 John 3:6)

- *"We know that whoever is born of God does not sin; but he who has been born of God keeps himself, and the wicked one does not touch him."* (1 John 5:18)

Why I wrote this book

This book has been necessitated by my long-term observation of various preachers from diverse church denominations on television, radio and other media in line with my intention of getting to know what is happening in other churches. I have been greatly disappointed by many of them and wonder how such preaching could ever convert people to become children of God. Sin is hardly mentioned in most of their sermons, but sin is mankind's only problem and Jesus Christ came into the world to save us from it.

I am a saint psychist ordained and sent by God to preach the gospel to mankind. After fasting and praying without ceasing to Almighty God about my observations, God directed me to write this book as a preliminary message to mankind for the greater work to follow by the children of God, hence the title *"Divine Direction"*.

Churchgoers

All churchgoers in all church denominations aspire to become God's children so that when they die they go to heaven to be with God the Father. All the churchgoers are called by God but only very few are chosen. We are reminded of this in Matthew 20:16 *"For many are called, but few chosen."* Those who are chosen become the children of God and do not commit sin. They are the true Christians. Those who are not chosen continue in sin and never become full Christians; they remain nominal Christians until they die in their sin and go to hell.

The church

The church as a whole is the largest institution in the world, and I find it pathetic that the church produces the worst results among all the institutions in existence. Many people are called by God to go to church to become his children, but unfortunately very few are chosen. Those chosen obey God absolutely and fear falling back into sin. You should not be surprised to read here, as directed by God, that only ten percent are chosen.

The reality of God, heaven and hell

This book serves to affirm the reality of God, heaven and hell as attested to by my mentor, Thearc Daniel Kingsley Arthur, the leader and founder of Thearchical Domain Church, who saw God in the middle of the night on 23 December 1952. His spirit was taken to see hell which he describes as a very dark place, overcrowded with people standing such that one was stepping upon another's foot and would not apologise.

His spirit was also taken to see heaven paradise which is the fourth of the seven heavens. According to him, the light there is the moon and he saw Martin Luther in the balcony of his room. This is the paradise where the spirit of Paul was taken to in his vision as retold in 2 Corinthians 12:4, *"I was caught up to paradise and heard things so astounding that they cannot be expressed in words."*

Finally, the spirit of Thearc Daniel was taken to the sixth heaven which is called the psychic realm or soul heaven. Jesus Christ hinted of this when he acknowledged John the Baptist in Matthew 11:11, *"Assuredly, I say to you, among those born of women there has not risen one greater than John the Baptist; but he who is least in the kingdom of heaven is greater than he."* John the Baptist and all other children of God who have already died are now in paradise, the fourth heaven. They are the second-class saints who will go to the sixth heaven which is the kingdom of heaven during the first resurrection of all saints. This is the place Jesus Christ referred to when He stated in John 14:2-3 *"In My Father's house are many mansions; if it were not so, I would have told you. I go to prepare a place for you. And if I go and prepare a place for you, I will come again and receive you to Myself; that where I am, there you may be also."*

Conclusion

The book focuses on the following teachings of the Holy Bible:

1. The only way to go to heaven is through being sinless. When a person knows that he does not commit sin God knows it too because sin separates one from God. Satan would also know it because it is Satan who makes one sin.

2. The only way to be sinless is to become a child of God.

3. The only way to be a child of God is to receive the Holy Spirit.

4. The only way to receive the Holy Spirit is to be born again.

5. The only way to be born again is when a person sent by God preaches and one repents, believes and has their belief affirmed by baptism, either by water or Spirit.

6. The only enemy mankind has is Satan because Satan is the only source of sin, so any sin committed by a person is caused by Satan.

7. The only problem mankind has is sin because sin is the only entity that separates mankind from God as stated in Isaiah 59:2, *"But your iniquities have separated you from your God; And your sins have hidden His face from you, so that He will not hear."*

Hence Jesus Christ came to the world to conquer Satan, our enemy, and to save us from our sins – our problem – so that whoever believes in Jesus Christ becomes a child of God like Him, and therefore does not commit sin. Whoever continues to sin is not a child of God, and therefore does not have the Holy Spirit to enable him to go to heaven. At death one goes to heaven with the Holy Spirit or to hell without the Holy Spirit. There is no middle way.

CHAPTER 1

THE CHURCH

Religion is a belief in God or gods. Christianity is the Christian religion which is a belief in the Almighty God only and is based on Jesus Christ, the only begotten Son of God and the only saviour and mediator between God the Father and sinful man.

The church is a congregation of people of the same belief in God through Jesus Christ. There are various denominations, and examples are Catholic, Presbyterian, Methodist, Anglican, Apostolic, Baptist, Assembly of God, Pentecostal and Thearchical Domain.

The church is the supreme institution where people of the same belief in God are taught to become Christians and therefore children of God.

The church is seen as the body of Christ with Him as the head. Jesus is the head of the local church of the congregation of both saved and unsaved believers. He is also the head of the universal church which is the spiritual church where all born again Christians, the saved of all the local churches, belong. This excludes the unsaved Christians of all the local churches. The universal church is also called the invisible church of God because the members do not congregate or meet physically as that is done in local churches.

The church is the largest institution in the world and yet it produces the worst results because only about ten percent of all the combined congregations qualify to go to heaven which is the ultimate goal of the church members.

The Holy Bible is the only prescribed book. The authors are God the Father, Jesus Christ the Son, and the Holy Spirit the comforter, and therefore the Trinity is the only interpreter of the Holy Bible. For one to understand and interpret the Holy Bible accurately, a Christian must of necessity have the Holy Spirit in him. The lessons of the Holy Bible are moral, spiritual and psychic based on the body, spirit and soul.

The instructors in the church are teachers and include the priests, pastors, ministers, apostles, bishops, deacons and evangelists. They form the clergy — the body of all people ordained for religious duties. The basic qualification of a church instructor is to be a born-again, Holy Spirit-filled Christian, called and sent by God for the work. The instructor's life should therefore be beyond reproach.

The main reason why, on average, all the churches in the world produce about ten percent true Christians and ninety percent nominal Christians is that most of the preachers have not been ordained and sent by God as stated in Romans 10:15 *"and how shall they preach, unless they are sent"* by God.

The preachers sent by God lay emphasis on sin as mankind's main problem, and explain that to overcome it one must be born again, receive the Holy Spirit and live a sinless life in order to go to heaven. The qualities of preachers ordained and sent by God are that they are blameless in conduct; do not take any strong drink; each have one spouse; are of good behaviour, vigilant and sober; are not quarrelsome; are capable of teaching; will not use wrong methods to make money; are patient; are not contentious; are quiet and peaceable; are not covetous; are not lovers of money, desiring the office for personal gain; are rulers of their own houses; and are not novices but get a good report from outsiders as well.

Preachers ordained and sent by God preach and convert some congregants to become true Christians whose attributes are holiness, righteousness, sinlessness, loving God and others, hating nobody, walking as Christ walked in the light and keeping all the commandments of God leading to eternal life.

It is the responsibility of the church to provide spiritual and physical guidance and support to the members. For spiritual guidance, the elders of the church must choose appropriate preachers sent by God to preach through prayers and periods of fasting. It is through such preachers that the true word of God will be preached for the members of the church to repent of their sins and be converted, after which they are baptised to receive the Holy Ghost to become true Christians.

The next responsibility of the church is to see to it that the unmarried marry to avoid fornication which is the most serious sin and one of the most common. The church must have rules and regulations governing marriage. As stated in 1 Corinthians 7:2, *"Nevertheless, because of sexual immorality, let each man have his own wife, and let each woman have her own husband."* The marriage law of the church should make it easy for members to marry. As much as possible, members should be encouraged to marry among members of the same congregation to keep the same faith and baptism. Where the two potential spouses happen to come from two different churches, there must be prayers and fasting and a calling to bring the two to attend the same church.

It is the responsibility of the church to support the needy members to obtain the basic things required to enable them to serve God well. It is imperative that every member capable of paying tithes does so because such tithes will enable the church to pay their expenditure including the costs of helping the needy.

The church is a spiritual family where the members are supported to form a congregation of saints as it is written in Ephesians 5:3 *"But fornication and all uncleanness or covetousness, let it not even be named among you, as is fitting for saints."* Jesus describes this to followers in Matthew 12:48-50: *"But He answered and said to the one who told Him, 'Who is My mother and who are My brothers?' And He stretched out His hand towards His disciples and said, 'Here are My mother and My brothers! For whoever does the will of My Father in heaven is My brother and sister and mother.'"* The church should acknowledge the importance of the spiritual family for it is in this family that members encourage one another to go to heaven.

The church should show interest in the education of the youth in the congregation and offer support where necessary. The aged, the widows and the widowers are to be encouraged and supported where required.

Jesus stated in Luke 4:18, *"The Spirit of the Lord is upon me, because he has anointed me to preach the gospel to the poor; he has sent me to heal the broken hearted, to proclaim liberty to the captives and recovery of sight to the blind, to set at liberty those who are oppressed."* Every preacher sent by God has been anointed to preach the gospel in the same way Christ was sent. The basic function of the church is to be involved in every facet of the life of the believer.

"Therefore take heed to yourselves and to all the flock, among which the Holy Spirit has made you overseers, to shepherd the church of God which He purchased with His own blood." (Acts 20:28)

"The church is called the home of God." (1 Timothy 3:15)

Conclusion

The ultimate aim of the church is to get members born again to become God's children and qualify to go to heaven. To achieve this, the church should appoint only preachers sent by God to preach the gospel. They should preach for the members to repent of their sins, be converted and baptised to receive the Holy Spirit.

Sinlessness must be emphasised in every preaching. The basic principle of the church should include daily readings of the Holy Bible, committing into memory some appropriate psalms and passages, praying unceasingly and observing weekly fasting and other special periods of fasting for spiritual upliftment.

"Therefore take heed to yourselves and to all the flock, among which the Holy Spirit has made you overseers, to shepherd the church of God which He purchased with His own blood." (Acts 20:28)

"The church is called the home of God." (1 Timothy 3:15)

CHAPTER 2

WHO IS A CHRISTIAN?

There are two types of Christians – true (real) Christians and false (nominal) Christians.

A true Christian is one who accepts his sins, genuinely repents, confesses, forsakes (leaves) his sins and genuinely believes in God by accepting the lordship of Jesus Christ.

A false Christian is one who accepts his sins, partially repents, confesses, partially forsakes his sins and partially believes in God.

Proverbs 28:13 states that *"He who covers his sins will not prosper, But whoever confesses and forsakes them will have mercy."*

A true Christian confesses (acknowledges) and forsakes (leaves) all his sins whereas a false Christian confesses but does not forsake (leave) all his sins.

A true Christian is one whose sins are forgiven by Christ and, because of his genuine belief, Christ takes away all the sins done in the past and comes to live in him.

A true Christian is a child of God who should not deliberately sin because the Holy Spirit dwells in him. This is confirmed by the following passages:

- *"Now he who keeps His commandments abides in Him, and He in him. And by this we know that He abides in us, by the Spirit whom He has given us."* (1 John 3:24)

- *"Whoever abides in Him does not sin. Whoever sins has neither seen Him nor known Him."* (1 John 3:6)

A Christian is one who has gone through two types of birth — the natural, physical birth, born by the union of man and woman, and the supernatural, spiritual birth, born by God. The birth by God (receiving the Holy Spirit) is the second birth, and is what Jesus Christ referred to as being *"born again"*.

Jesus elaborates on it as follows:

- *"Unless one is born again, he cannot see the kingdom of God."* (John 3:3)

- *"Unless one is born of water and the Spirit, he cannot enter the kingdom of God."* (John 3:5)

- *"That which is born of the flesh is flesh; and that which is born of the Spirit is spirit."* (John 3:6)

A true Christian is one who is born again — born of God — and therefore cannot wilfully sin as affirmed below:

- *"Whoever has been born of God does not sin, for His seed remains in him; and he cannot sin, because he has been born of God."* (1 John 3:9)

- *"We know that whoever is born of God does not sin; but he who has been born of God keeps himself, and the wicked one does not touch him."* (1 John 5:18)

- *"My little children, these things I write to you, so that you may not sin. And if anyone sins, we have an Advocate with the Father, Jesus Christ the righteous."* (1 John 2:1)

This also confirms that a Christian should not sin, but in case a Christian does sin, which could be unintentional, then we have Jesus to intercede on our behalf.

In two instances Jesus forgave sinners but warned them and gave the instruction, *"go and sin no more"*.

- In John 5:1-14, with regard to the man who had an infirmity for 38 years and who Jesus met in Jerusalem at Bethesda by the pool at the sheep gate, Jesus healed him and later on met him in the temple and warned him *"go and sin no more"* lest worse things came upon him.

- *In John 8:1-11 we read of a woman caught in adultery and brought to Jesus by the scribes and Pharisees. Jesus forgave her but warned her "go and sin no more".*

The instruction from Jesus to true Christians is that we should not sin anymore because He has saved us and wants to prevent worse things happening to us.

Jesus affirms the true Christians as follows:

- *"I am the good shepherd; and I know My sheep, and am known by My own."* (John 10:14)

- *"My sheep hear My voice, and I know them, and they follow Me."* (John 10:27)

True Christians are therefore those who hear the word of God and rigidly adhere to what it says.

A true Christian is one who is saved by grace through a genuine faith in God, leading to him being given the Holy Spirit. A genuine faith is built on trust, and what follows trust is obedience which is the keeping of the commandments of God.

John 14:15 tells us, *"If you love Me, keep My commandments."*

John 14:21 states, *"He who has My commandments and keeps them, it is he who loves Me. And he who loves Me will be loved by My Father, and I will love him and manifest Myself to him."*

Since a true Christian should not sin because of the Holy Spirit in him, a Christian keeps all the commandments of God because all the commandments instruct us not to sin. This confirms that a true Christian loves God.

A true Christian is one who is not under the law but under grace. A true Christian is under grace because it is by grace, through a genuine belief in God, that he is saved to obtain the Holy Spirit. Because of this the true Christian seeks righteousness, which is the righteousness in Christ through grace and belief. A true Christian is not under the law but above the law because, thanks to grace, he inherently and naturally keeps all the laws and would not think of doing anything wrong. The law becomes irrelevant to the true Christian because he has taken care of it already.

Galatians 5:18 states, *"But if you are led by the Spirit, you are not under the law."*

This means that because a true Christian has the Spirit of God living in him, he inherently keeps the commandments of God because he is led by the Spirit of God and therefore is not under the law.

In I John 5:3 we're told: *"For this is the love of God, that we keep His commandments. And His commandments are not burdensome."* It is not difficult or grievous for the true Christians to obey the commandments because of the Holy Spirit in them, but it is difficult and grievous for the false Christians to do so because they do not have the Spirit of God to grant them power to keep the commandments.

A true Christian is inherently righteous and holy through God's grace, the belief in Jesus Christ and the Holy Spirit given him by God. This is affirmed by I Timothy 1:9 which says, *"Knowing this: that the law is not made for a righteous person, but for the lawless and insubordinate, for the ungodly and for sinners, for the unholy and profane, for murderers of fathers and murderers of mothers, for manslayers."*

In Matthew 7:21 Jesus said, *"Not everyone who says to Me, 'Lord, Lord,' shall enter the kingdom of heaven, but he who does the will of My Father in heaven."*

A true Christian does the will of God by obeying Him by keeping His commandments. Many people call on the name of God while praising, fasting, praying, and reading the Bible, but not all of them obey God absolutely. It is only those who obey God absolutely that are true Christians and qualify to go to heaven. In Matthew 22:14 Jesus said this: *"For many are called, but few are chosen."*

Indeed, those who say *"Lord, Lord"* while praising, fasting, fellowshipping and praying to God are called by God, but only those who strictly obey God by keeping His commandments are the true Christians chosen and qualified to go to heaven.

In James 1:22 we read, *"But be ye doers of the word, and not hearers only, deceiving your own selves."* A true Christian is one who, after hearing the word of God, puts it into practice by obeying it as required. A false Christian is one who hears the word of God but does not obey it. Such a Christian is deceiving himself by claiming to be born again.

A genuine Christian is one who intentionally does what is right and unintentionally does what is wrong. But a false Christian is one who intentionally does what is right and what is wrong. Such a Christian serves both God and mammon (riches or material wealth) but God is a jealous god, who does not share His love.

A true Christian is one who regularly fasts for spiritual upliftment. A genuine Christian does not wait until problems arise before fasting. Fasting is compulsory for Christians. Jesus did it and so did all the great men of God including Moses, Joshua, David, Daniel, other prophets and prophetesses as well as the apostles of Jesus.

In Matthew 6:16-17 Jesus said, *"Moreover, when you fast, do not be like the hypocrites, with a sad countenance. But you, when you fast, anoint your head and wash your face."* Husband and wife are advised in 1 Corinthians 7:5, *"Do not deprive one another except with consent for a time, that you may give yourselves to fasting and prayer; and come together again so that Satan does not tempt you because of your lack of self-control."*

A true Christian is one whose body is the temple of God and the kingdom of God and therefore he cannot wilfully sin with any part of the body.

A true Christian is spiritually minded and consults God in every decision taken and hence finds it difficult to sin because God is involved in all aspects of his life.

A true Christian is one who forgives immediately when offended without any precondition, like waiting for an apology from the offender, bearing in mind how he has tasted the real forgiveness from God.

A true Christian is one whose anger is brief, because prolonged anger is a sin and Satan capitalises on it to block a Christian's communication with God. The more mature a Christian is in the spirit, the quicker he'll get over his anger.

The following passages confirm this stance.

"Be angry, and do not sin: do not let the sun go down on your wrath." (Ephesians 4:26)

"Agree with your adversary quickly, while you are on the way with him, lest your adversary deliver you to the judge, the judge hand you over to the officer, and you be thrown into prison." (Matthew 5:25)

A true Christian pays tithes. It is imperative; it is a command. It is like stealing from God if you don't pay tithes, and whosoever steals will not inherit the kingdom of heaven.

Malachi 3:9-10 says, "'*You are cursed with a curse, for you have robbed Me, even this whole nation. Bring all the tithes into the storehouse, that there may be food in My house, and try Me now in this,' says the Lord of hosts, 'If I will not open for you the windows of heaven and pour out for you such blessing that there will not be room enough to receive it.'*"

A true Christian is someone who has been crucified with Christ. Galatians 2:20 says "*It is no longer I who live, but Christ lives in me; and the life which I now live in the flesh I live by faith in the Son of God, who loved me and gave Himself for me.*"

A true Christian is someone who, as mentioned in Romans 6:18, "*having been set free from sin, you became slaves of righteousness.*"

A true Christian has at least one of the nine gifts of the Holy Spirit because of the Holy Spirit living in him. The gifts are wisdom, knowledge, faith, healing, miracles, prophecy, discerning of spirits, speaking in tongues and interpretation of tongues.

A true Christian may lose the Holy Spirit through intentional sins like fornication and adultery, because the Holy Spirit leaves the body before it is polluted by the person's sin. This is affirmed by Psalm 51:11 which states, "*Do not cast me away from Your presence, and do not take Your Holy Spirit from me.*" A false Christian has nothing to lose because he never had the Holy Spirit.

A true Christian is one who is qualified to preach the gospel to convert sinners because of the Holy Spirit living in him. This is confirmed by Psalm 51:12-13 which says, "*Restore to me the joy of Your salvation, and uphold me by Your generous Spirit. Then I will teach transgressors Your ways, and sinners shall be converted to You.*" And in Acts 1:8 we're told, "*But you shall receive power when the Holy Spirit has come upon you; and you shall be witnesses to Me in Jerusalem, and in all Judea and Samaria, and to the end of the earth.*"

Luke 24:49 repeats the above when Jesus told the disciples after the resurrection, "*Behold, I send the Promise of My Father upon you; but tarry in the city of Jerusalem until you are endued with power from on high.*" A true Christian has the Holy Spirit in him and is therefore endowed with power to witness for God.

A true Christian should not intentionally commit even one sin because the Holy Bible tells us in James 2:10-11, "*For whoever shall keep the whole law, and yet stumble in one point, he is guilty of all. For He who said 'Do not commit adultery' also said 'Do not murder'. Now if you do not commit adultery, but you do murder, you have become a transgressor of the law."* A single sin in one's life is disobedience to God and leads to hell if it's not stopped. A true Christian is therefore sinless which is the only way for one to qualify to go to heaven.

In Hebrews 9:28 we're told, *"So Christ was offered once to bear the sins of many. To those who eagerly wait for Him He will appear a second time, apart from sin, for salvation."* This confirms the second coming of Christ. Christ has come for the second time in the form of the Holy Spirit living in the true Christians to do the greater work. This is therefore the time that only those who are without sin obtain salvation.

A true Christian is one who is pure in heart, humble, merciful, peaceful, harmless, slow to anger, slow to speak, quick to hear and able to endure all types of persecution.

Matthew 5:44 tells us: *"But I say to you, love your enemies, bless those who curse you, do good to those who hate you, and pray for those who spitefully use you and persecute you."*

According to 2 Corinthians 5:20, *"We are ambassadors for Christ, as though God were pleading through us: we implore you on Christ's behalf, be reconciled to God."*

Conclusion

Christ came to show us the way to God, so He is the way. We all try to imitate Christ — what He did is what we try to do, and we say what He said. In so doing we may end up being good Christians.

A real Christian is the one who accepts Christ as Lord and Saviour and follows Him.

A nominal Christian is the one who accepts Christ but does not follow Him.

A non-Christian does not accept Christ and does not follow Him.

A real Christian will start by embracing the attitudes and behaviour Jesus wants of His followers — the beatitudes. As he or she accepts Christ and follows Him, he or she becomes like salt to preserve and light to shine, a teacher and keeper of truth. He or she becomes free from hypocrisy, selfishness and grudges — a family man/woman, charitable and neighbourly in society.

To be a Christian is to be Christ-like, showing the way to God. The way to God is through the cross which Christ bore which symbolically means uprightness. We cannot please God if we do not love him, and we cannot love him if we do not love our neighbour. We love a neighbour when we help him or her go to heaven. The whole duty of a Christian is to win souls for God, for as we read in Proverbs 11:30, *"The fruit of the righteous is a tree of life, And he who wins souls is wise."*

CHAPTER 3

WARNINGS TO TRUE CHRISTIANS

A true Christian is a person who has the Holy Spirit living in him. As soon as the Holy Spirit is taken away from him through sin he ceases to be a true Christian and a child of God.

Psalm 51:11 says *"Do not cast me away from Your presence, and do not take Your Holy Spirit from me."* When the Holy Spirit leaves the body it goes with its power and light so that the body is empty and now engulfed in darkness. Since Satan is aware when a person receives or loses the Holy Spirit, Satan now takes control and uses the person to do evil deeds.

Psalm 51:11 is part of the prayer offered by David when he committed adultery, and it's the most serious warning to the true Christian. If a true Christian, filled with the Holy Ghost, fornicates or commits adultery the Holy Spirit is taken away from him. The Holy Spirit leaves the body prior to the committing of the sin. It takes appropriate guidance for the restoration of the Holy Ghost. David again confirms this in the next verse, Psalm 51:12, *"Restore to me the joy of Your salvation, and uphold me by Your generous Spirit."*

However, in Hebrews 6:4-6 we read, *"For it is impossible for those who were once enlightened, and have tasted the heavenly gift, and have become partakers of the Holy Spirit, and have tasted the good word of God and the powers of the age to come, if they fall away, to renew them again to repentance, since they crucify again for themselves the Son of God, and put Him to an open shame."*

Since true Christians are partakers of the Holy Spirit, the above serious warning is applicable to them. Should a true Christian indulge in sin it may lead to him losing the Holy Spirit and not getting it back again.

Hebrews 10:26-29 says, *"For if we sin wilfully after we have received the knowledge of the truth, there no longer remains a sacrifice for sins, but a certain fearful expectation of judgment, and fiery indignation which will devour the adversaries. Anyone who has rejected Moses' law dies without mercy on the testimony of two or three witnesses. Of how much worse punishment, do you suppose, will he be thought worthy who has trampled the Son of God underfoot, counted the blood of the covenant by which he was sanctified a common thing, and insulted the Spirit of grace?"*

A true Christian is one who should not sin wilfully because he has the Holy Spirit living in him. The above passage is one of the strong warnings to true Christians that if they sin wilfully they will lose the Holy Spirit, and the consequence is very serious — a fearful judgment.

Another warning to true Christians is found in 2 Peter 2:20-21 which states, *"For if, after they have escaped the pollutions of the world through the knowledge of the Lord and Saviour Jesus Christ, they are again entangled in them and overcome, the latter end is worse for them than the beginning. For it would have been better for them not to have known the way of righteousness, than having known it, to turn from the holy commandment delivered to them."*

Indeed, a true Christian has escaped the pollution of the world by not committing sin because of the Holy Spirit in him. The serious warning is that, should a Christian go back into the world to pollute himself by sinning again, the things that happen to him could be worse than before he was born again.

A true Christian is righteous and therefore knows the way of righteousness and the holy commandments which he has been keeping, so turning away from them is a wilful sin which is so serious that he could lose the Holy Spirit.

A true Christian would do well to pray Psalm 19:13 which reads: *"Keep back Your servant also from presumptuous sins; Let them not have dominion over me. Then I shall be blameless, and I shall be innocent of great transgression."*

This verse emphasises the seriousness of a true Christian committing a wilful sin. This is a great transgression and therefore a serious sin which could lead to him forfeiting the Holy Spirit.

Matthew 10:22 emphasises that *"he who endures to the end will be saved"*. It is therefore essential for a true Christian to continue to obey God to the very end before he can be certain of being saved to enter into the kingdom of God.

In Hebrews 3:6 we read *"But Christ as a Son over His own house, whose house we are if we hold fast the confidence and the rejoicing of the hope firm to the end."*

The body of any true Christian is the temple of God and therefore the house belonging to Christ. The house will continue to belong to Christ only if we hold fast to our confidence and rejoice in this hope firmly unto the end. A true Christian can only live with Christ if he does only that which pleases Christ and that requires obedience to God.

Hebrews 3:13-14 encourages us to *"exhort one another daily, while it is called 'Today', lest any of you be hardened through the deceitfulness of sin. For we have become partakers of Christ if we hold the beginning of our confidence steadfast to the end."*

A true Christian has Christ in him and continues to be with Christ if he holds fast with confidence from the time he was born again to the end of his life and is careful not to be deceived by sin.

Judas Iscariot was one of Jesus Christ's apostles and was undoubtedly born again otherwise he would not have been commissioned along with the other apostles to go and preach the kingdom of God to people. Yet because of his love of money Satan enticed Judas to betray Jesus for only thirty pieces of silver. In the same way Satan entices born again Christians to sin and thus lose the Holy Ghost. This is a major lesson and warning to any true Christian.

In Revelation 2:10 Jesus tells true Christians, *"Be faithful until death, and I will give you the crown of life."*

A true Christian is encouraged to be faithful unto death in order to go to heaven to receive a crown. Failure to be faithful to God to the end will lead to Christians forfeiting the Holy Spirit and losing access to heaven.

More warnings to Christians are stated in the following verses:

- *"Therefore we must give the more earnest heed to the things we have heard, lest we drift away."* (Hebrews 2:1)

- *"How shall we escape if we neglect so great a salvation, which at the first began to be spoken by the Lord, and was confirmed to us by those who heard Him."* (Hebrews 2:3)

- *"Beware, brethren, lest there be in any of you an evil heart of unbelief in departing from the living God."* (Hebrews 3:12)

- *"Seeing then that we have a great High Priest who has passed through the heavens, Jesus the Son of God, let us hold fast our confession."* (Hebrews 4:14)

- "And we desire that each one of you show the same diligence to the full assurance of hope until the end." (Hebrews 6:11)

- "Let us hold fast the confession of our hope without wavering, for He who promised is faithful." (Hebrews 10:23)

- "Therefore do not cast away your confidence, which has great reward." (Hebrews 10:35)

- "'Now the just shall live by faith; But if anyone draws back, My soul has no pleasure in him.' But we are not of those who draw back to perdition, but of those who believe to the saving of the soul." (Hebrews 10:38-39)

- "Therefore we also, since we are surrounded by so great a cloud of witnesses, let us lay aside every weight, and the sin which so easily ensnares us, and let us run with endurance the race that is set before us, looking unto Jesus, the author and finisher of our faith." (Hebrews 12:1-2)

- "Looking carefully lest anyone fall short of the grace of God; lest any root of bitterness springing up cause trouble, and by this many become defiled; lest there be any fornicator or profane person like Esau, who for one morsel of food sold his birthright." (Hebrews 12:15-16)

- "Therefore, since we are receiving a kingdom which cannot be shaken, let us have grace, by which we may serve God acceptably with reverence and godly fear. For our God is a consuming fire." (Hebrews 12:28-29)

- "The righteousness of the righteous shall not deliver him in the day of his transgression." (Ezekiel 33:12)

- "When the righteous turns from his righteousness and commits iniquity, he shall die because of it." (Ezekiel 33:18)

The warning that Jesus Christ gave when he healed the sick and forgave the sins of sinners was this: Go and sin no more, lest worse things should happen unto you. This warning still applies to all true Christians because Jesus Christ's forgiveness of sin is made real by all true Christians who no longer sin intentionally.

Conclusion

The above warnings are enough to conclude that a true Christian who has the Holy Spirit dwelling in him can lose the Holy Spirit through sin and that his failure to be faithful to God to the end will lead to him forfeiting his access to the kingdom of heaven.

CHAPTER 4

WARNINGS TO CHURCHGOERS

Churchgoers are those who go to church regularly with the intent of becoming Christians, but most of them never become true Christians but remain as nominal Christians, and then they die and go to hell. Only a few of them truly become Christians and remain that way until they die and go to heaven.

The majority of the churchgoers are nominal Christians or false Christians and only a small minority of the churchgoers are real Christians or true Christians. Nominal Christians are not born again because they do not have the Holy Spirit living in them and therefore continue to sin deliberately, but the real Christians are born again and have the Holy Spirit living in them, so they should not sin deliberately.

Distinguishing between nominal Christians and real Christians

"Many are called, but few chosen." (Matthew 20:16) Whoever goes to church is called by God, but only a few of those are chosen and have the Holy Spirit living in them. These people obey God and do not sin deliberately. A large number are not chosen because they continue to sin deliberately.

"Not everyone who says to Me, 'Lord, Lord,' shall enter the kingdom of heaven, but he who does the will of My Father in heaven." (Matthew 7:21) All churchgoers call upon God, praying and praising Him, but a large number of them are nominal Christians who do not do the will of God; they continue to sin and therefore shall not go to heaven. Only the small number of them who obey Him by doing God's will enter into the kingdom of heaven.

"But be doers of the word, and not hearers only, deceiving yourselves." (James 1:22) The vast majority of churchgoers are nominal Christians who hear the word of God but do not obey absolutely and therefore are deceiving themselves and cannot go to heaven. Only the small number of churchgoers who hear and obey God and please God can enter the kingdom of heaven.

"Enter by the narrow gate; for wide is the gate and broad is the way that leads to destruction, and there are many who go in by it. Because narrow is the gate and difficult is the way which leads to life, and there are few who find it." (Matthew 7:13-14) A large number of churchgoers – the nominal Christians – are on the broad way which leads to destruction. Only a few churchgoers – the true Christians – are on the narrow way which leads to eternal life.

"For whoever shall keep the whole law, and yet stumble in one point, he is guilty of all. For He who said, 'Do not commit adultery,' also said, 'Do not murder'. Now if you do not commit adultery, but you do murder, you have become a transgressor of the law." (James 2:10-11) A great number of churchgoers have at least one sin which they know about and yet continue to commit. This is still disobedience to God and therefore it's regarded as if all sins are committed which is also disobedience to God. Only a minimal number of churchgoers do not commit any sin, obey God absolutely and are therefore the children of God and real Christians.

"Whoever abides in Him does not sin. Whoever sins has neither seen Him nor known Him." (1 John 3:6) Since the majority of churchgoers continue in sin, they do not abide in God and therefore they have not seen him or known him. Only the minority that dwell in God have seen him and known him and do not commit any sin.

"Whoever has been born of God does not sin, for His seed remains in him; and he cannot sin, because he has been born of God." (1 John 3:9) The vast majority of churchgoers commit sin and therefore they are not born of God and do not have the Holy Spirit. A tiny minority of churchgoers do not commit sin because they are born of God and the Holy Spirit lives in them.

"Now he who keeps His commandments abides in Him, and He in him. And by this we know that He abides in us, by the Spirit whom He has given us." (1 John 3:24) The vast majority of churchgoers do not keep all the commandments; they continue to sin and therefore they do not dwell in God and God does not dwell in them either and they are not given the Holy Spirit. A tiny minority of churchgoers keep all the commandments of God and therefore dwell in Him and He in them, and have this confirmed by the Holy Spirit which God gives them.

"We know that whoever is born of God does not sin; but he who has been born of God keeps himself, and the wicked one does not touch him." (1 John 5:18) The vast majority of churchgoers who continue to commit sin cannot claim to be children of God and therefore Satan has access to them. The true born-again Christians do not commit sin and therefore Satan cannot touch them.

"My little children, these things I write to you, so that you may not sin. And if anyone sins, we have an Advocate with the Father, Jesus Christ the righteous." (1 John 2:1) The few churchgoers who are the children of God do not commit sin intentionally, but if it happens abruptly or unknowingly and they repent, Jesus intervenes with the Father to ensure their forgiveness. But the large percentage of churchgoers who sin deliberately do not have Christ to intervene for them until they repent genuinely and become God's children.

"If we say that we have fellowship with Him, and walk in darkness, we lie and do not practice the truth." (1 John 1:6) This refers to the majority of churchgoers who claim to have fellowship with God, but who are actually lying because they still walk in darkness as long as they disobey God by regularly sinning.

"Now by this we know that we know Him, if we keep His commandments." (1 John 2:3) A large percentage of churchgoers do not keep all the commandments and therefore do not know God. A small percentage of churchgoers keep all the commandments because they do not commit any sin and therefore know God.

"He who says, 'I know Him,' and does not keep His commandments, is a liar, and the truth is not in him." (1 John 2:4) All churchgoers claim to know God, but those who do not keep all the commandments are lying, and deceiving themselves.

"If you know that He is righteous, you know that everyone who practices righteousness is born of Him." (1 John 2:29) All churchgoers know that God is righteous and that only those who are righteous are the children of God, and yet a large percentage of these churchgoers are unrighteous because they are nominal Christians and only a small percentage are real Christians and righteous because they are born of God.

"I have been crucified with Christ; it is no longer I who live, but Christ lives in me; and the life which I now live in the flesh I live by faith in the Son of God, who loved me and gave Himself for me." (Galatians 2:20) Most churchgoers do not have Christ living in them because they continue to live in sin. Only a small minority of churchgoers have Christ living in them and live a Christ-like life.

"For you were once darkness, but now you are light in the Lord. Walk as children of light." (Ephesians 5:8) The vast majority of churchgoers are still in darkness because they continue to sin. It is only a few churchgoers who are no longer in darkness but in the light in the Lord and walk as children of light because they are born again, spirit filled and sinless.

"But as He who called you is holy, you also be holy in all your conduct, because it is written, 'Be holy, for I am holy.'" (1 Peter 1:15-16) All churchgoers are called by God to be holy but the majority of those called are still not holy, because they continue to disobey God by their sins and only a few of those called are holy because they obey God and commit no sin because of the Holy Spirit in them.

"For he will be great in the sight of the Lord, and shall drink neither wine nor strong drink. He will also be filled with the Holy Spirit, even from his mother's womb." (Luke 1:15) Here the angel Gabriel announced the conception and birth of John the Baptist to Zachariah, John's father, telling him that the Holy Spirit and alcohol are incompatible. Many churchgoers take strong drink and therefore cannot have the Holy Spirit living in them.

"Or do you not know that your body is the temple of the Holy Spirit who is in you, whom you have from God, and you are not your own?" (1 Corinthians 6:19) Whoever takes alcohol or smokes or fornicates or does any unclean thing cannot have the Holy Spirit living in him because his body is unholy. A large percentage of churchgoers are guilty of at least one of them.

"Now then, we are ambassadors for Christ, as though God were pleading through us: we implore you on Christ's behalf, be reconciled to God." (2 Corinthians 5:20) The vast majority of churchgoers cannot be ambassadors of Christ because Christ never sinned, but they continue to sin. Only a few churchgoers are true ambassadors of Christ because they are like Christ since they do not sin.

"All unrighteousness is sin, and there is sin not leading to death." (1 John 5:17) Any unrighteous deed done deliberately is sin, so a huge percentage of churchgoers are unrighteous because they continue to sin. Only a small percentage of churchgoers are righteous because they do not commit sin.

"Jesus answered and said unto him, 'Verily, verily, I say unto thee, Except a man be born again, he cannot see the kingdom of God' ... Jesus answered, 'Verily, verily, I say unto thee, Except a man be born of water and of the Spirit, he cannot enter into the kingdom of God.'" (John 3:3; 5) Most churchgoers are not born again — they are born of water, the physical birth, but not born of the spirit, the spiritual birth by which God grants the Holy Spirit. As a result they continue to sin and cannot enter into the kingdom of God. A few churchgoers

are born again, having undergone physical and spiritual birth, and therefore have the Holy Spirit in them which qualifies them to go to heaven.

"There is therefore now no condemnation to those who are in Christ Jesus, who do not walk according to the flesh, but according to the Spirit." (Romans 8:1) The majority of churchgoers do not have the Spirit of God living in them and therefore continue to sin and walk after the flesh and hence are condemned to hell. Only the small percentage of churchgoers who have the Spirit of God living in them and therefore walk after the spirit will not be condemned to hell.

"Do you not know that to whom you present yourselves slaves to obey, you are that one's slaves whom you obey, whether of sin leading to death, or of obedience leading to righteousness?" (Romans 6:16) All those churchgoers who continue to sin are therefore servants of sin and of Satan who they obey, and so death and hell is their end. Only the few churchgoers who obey God are servants of God which is obedience unto righteousness which leads to eternal life.

"For not the hearers of the law are just in the sight of God, but the doers of the law will be justified." (Romans 2:13) Only a small percentage of churchgoers are hearers and doers of the law and therefore justified before God, while the vast majority are hearers and not doers of the law and therefore unjustified before God.

"The devising of foolishness is sin." (Proverbs 24:9) Many, many churchgoers have foolish thoughts because they continue to sin and all sins come from foolish thoughts. The small percentage of churchgoers who have the Holy Spirit in them have godly thoughts.

"For as many as are led by the Spirit of God, these are sons of God." (Romans 8:14) Very few churchgoers really have the Spirit of God living in them and are therefore led by the Spirit of God and are the sons of God. Most churchgoers do not have the Spirit of God living in them and are therefore not led by the Spirit of God and are not the sons of God.

"If I regard iniquity in my heart, The Lord will not hear." (Psalm 66:18) A large percentage of churchgoers regard iniquity in their hearts because they continue to sin and hence the Lord does not hear them; the Lord hears only the small percentage of churchgoers who do not regard iniquity in their hearts.

"But your iniquities have separated you from your God; And your sins have hidden His face from you, So that He will not hear." (Isaiah 59:2) The iniquities of the vast majority of churchgoers have separated them from God and their sins

have hidden God's face from them so that God does not hear them when they pray. God only hears the minority of churchgoers who are true Christians because they obey God and therefore have no iniquities to separate them from God and no sins that would cause God to turn His face from them.

Conclusion

As divinely directed, about ninety percent of churchgoers do not have the Holy Spirit in them and continue in sin. They are therefore nominal Christians who wish to become true Christians but are not yet, and hence when they die in their sin and not in the Lord they go to hell. Only about ten percent of churchgoers are sinless and are true Christians, and when they die they die without sin and in the Lord and heaven is their eternal dwelling place.

Which of the two groups of churchgoers do you belong to? Are you a real Christian or a nominal Christian? A true Christian or a false Christian? Only God, you and Satan know.

CHAPTER 5

WHAT IS SIN?

Sin is disobedience to God. In 1 John 3:4 it is written: *"Whoever commits sin also commits lawlessness, and sin is lawlessness."* Whose law is transgressed? It is God's law. Sin is therefore going against God's law, and going against God's law is disobedience to God.

Satan was the first to disobey God, and therefore first to sin as is alluded to in Isaiah 14:13-14. Adam and Eve were the second to sin. They sinned in the Garden of Eden when they disobeyed God by eating the forbidden fruit as written in Genesis 3:3-6. Adam and Eve disobeyed God and obeyed Satan.

Sin is therefore disobedience to God or obedience to Satan or both.

Two types of sin

Sin can come in many ways and take many forms, but there are two broad types. There is sin of commission and sin of omission. A sin of commission is deliberately doing the wrong thing, while a sin of omission is deliberately not doing the right thing. James 4:17 says, *"Therefore, to him who knows to do good and does not do it, to him it is sin."*

Degrees of sin: Pardonable sin and unpardonable sin

Pardonable Sin

Under pardonable sin we have some very serious sins and other seemingly less serious sins.

Adultery and fornication are classified as very serious, as we're warned in 1 Corinthians 6:18-20 *"Flee sexual immorality. Every sin that a man does is outside the body, but he who commits sexual immorality sins against his own body. Or do you not know that your body is the temple of the Holy Spirit who is in you, whom you have from God, and you are not your own? For you were bought at a price; therefore glorify God in your body and in your spirit, which are God's."*

Fornication and adultery are the most serious sins and yet they are among the most common sins in the world. Before a true Christian who is filled with the Holy Spirit fornicates or commits adultery, the Holy Spirit leaves the body. It is taken away from the body by God. Hence when David committed adultery he rightly prayed to God *"Do not cast me away from Your presence, and do not take Your Holy Spirit from me"* (Psalm 51:11). When the Holy Spirit is taken away prior to fornication or adultery it takes appropriate guidance for it to be restored. Hence David continued in his prayer in Psalm 51:12 *"Restore to me the joy of Your salvation, and uphold me by Your generous Spirit."*

There are degrees of sin but every sin leads to condemnation and eternal death, for the wages of sin is death and if a person is guilty of one sin he is guilty of all sins.

Unpardonable Sin

Luke 12:10 states *"And anyone who speaks a word against the Son of Man, it will be forgiven him; but to him who blasphemes against the Holy Spirit, it will not be forgiven."*

In Hebrews 6:4-6 we read, *"For it is impossible for those who were once enlightened, and have tasted the heavenly gift, and have become partakers of the Holy Spirit, and have tasted the good word of God and the powers of the age to come, if they fall away, to renew them again to repentance, since they crucify again for themselves the Son of God, and put Him to an open shame."*

Hebrews 10:26-29 tells us, *"For if we sin wilfully after we have received the knowledge of the truth, there no longer remains a sacrifice for sins, but a certain fearful expectation of judgment, and fiery indignation which will devour the adversaries. Anyone who has rejected Moses' law dies without mercy on the testimony of two or three witnesses. Of how much worse punishment, do you suppose, will he be thought worthy who has trampled the Son of God underfoot, counted the blood of the covenant by which he was sanctified a common thing, and insulted the Spirit of grace?"*

WHAT IS SIN?

In 1 John 5:17 we read: *"All unrighteousness is sin"*, thus any wrongdoing done deliberately is sin. Any sin committed is first against God and second against the offended or victim. It is against God because any sin committed is disobedience to God.

Sin may be in thought, word or deed; it may be physical or spiritual.

The following passages are examples:

- *"The devising of foolishness is sin."* (Proverbs 24:9)

- *"He who despises his neighbour sins."* (Proverbs 14:21)

- *"For we know that the law is spiritual, but I am carnal, sold under sin."* (Romans 7:14)

- *"All unrighteousness is sin."* (1 John 5:17)

It is sin to be carnal, an unbeliever or worldly because anybody in this situation is unrighteous.

In Romans 14:23 we read, *"But he who doubts is condemned if he eats, because he does not eat from faith; for whatever is not from faith is sin."*

Our faith in God must take pre-eminence in whatever we do. If there is any doubt in what we do it means we are not full of faith and therefore it becomes a sin if we do

Ephesians 4:26 says, *"Be angry, and do not sin: do not let the sun go down on your wrath."* Anger by itself may not be sin because it can happen all of a sudden, but if it is prolonged it invariably leads to sin. In the same way, when one is tempted one has not sinned, but when one falls into that trap by acting it leads to sin.

Sin can be intentional or unintentional.

The intentional sin committed by a true Christian is regarded as very serious as stated in Hebrews 10:26 *"For if we sin wilfully after we have received the knowledge of the truth, there no longer remains a sacrifice for sins."*

James 1:15 states: *"Then, when desire has conceived, it gives birth to sin; and sin, when it is full-grown, brings forth death."*

Romans 6:23 says, *"For the wages of sin is death."*

Lust is the greatest temptation that leads to sin and sin is the only entity that leads to eternal death and which separates man from God.

Conclusion

Sin is disobedience to God or obedience to Satan or both. It is the only obstacle that separates one from God. Christ came into the world in order to conquer Satan and abolish sin. Anyone who genuinely believes in God has the grace of Christ, and with Christ living in him this person is able to conquer sin and live a sinless life.

CHAPTER 6

REPENTANCE

Repentance is an admission of guilt of the sins one has committed from childhood which one could not control, and realising the seriousness of that sin through hearing God's word preached by an anointed man of God, and being prepared to forgo worldliness through Satan for godliness through Jesus Christ.

Repentance is where one is penitent, regretful, remorseful, repentant and deeply sorry for all the past sins from birth, and genuinely decides to serve God for the rest of one's life after hearing the gospel through the correct teachings which convict one of their past sinful life.

Repentance is a spiritual exercise which leads to physical action. It is a change of heart and mind through hearing the word of God and is confirmed by a change in lifestyle from worldliness to godliness.

Genuine repentance involves a vow and spiritual covenant made between the repentant person and God that the repentant will be faithful to God to the end and not deliberately sin again.

It is a point of recognising the old nature of sinfulness which ruled the person since birth, and turning to the new nature of sinlessness which will rule them till death.

It is the most important decision every Christian takes — to serve only God and be godly and not worldly for the rest of their life. It requires a permanent change in character from worldliness to godliness and from sinfulness to sinlessness.

Scriptural emphasis on repentance

In Matthew 9:13 we read, *"But go and learn what this means: 'I desire mercy and not sacrifice.' For I did not come to call the righteous, but sinners, to repentance."* Here Jesus reminds us that his mission was to save sinners, and for one to be saved it is imperative that one repents which should lead to righteousness.

Why is it that there are so many preachers and so many people who go to church regularly, but only about ten percent of those who go to church genuinely repent, because about ninety percent still intentionally commit sin.

Sin is the only problem for mankind, and it's the reason why Jesus came to die to save us, and yet most preachers rarely mention sin in their preaching.

Jesus said in Mark 1:15, *"The time is fulfilled, and the kingdom of God is at hand. Repent, and believe in the gospel."* This means the kingdom of God is there for everybody, but for one to get it one must of necessity repent which makes one believe the gospel.

This is again emphasised in Luke 13:3 where Jesus says, *"I tell you, no; but unless you repent you will all likewise perish."* Repentance is compulsory for one to be born again, and whoever does not repent is bound to go to hell.

In Matthew 3:2 John the Baptist also preached, saying, *"Repent, for the kingdom of heaven is at hand!"*

Luke 3:8 tells us: *"Therefore bear fruits worthy of repentance, and do not begin to say to yourselves, 'We have Abraham as our father.' For I say to you that God is able to raise up children to Abraham from these stones."* If someone says they have repented it should be confirmed by the fruit being borne in the life they live. We cannot just claim that we are Abraham's seed, we must repent.

Acts 3:19 says, *"Repent therefore and be converted, that your sins may be blotted out, so that times of refreshing may come from the presence of the Lord."*

Repentance should lead to conversion, and after conversion one's sins are forgiven, so one should sin no more. Continuing to sin means one is not born again.

Acts 2:38 states *"Then Peter said to them, 'Repent, and let every one of you be baptised in the name of Jesus Christ for the remission of sins; and you shall receive the gift of the Holy Spirit.'"* It is after repentance that one is baptised which leads to forgiveness of sin and the granting of the Holy Ghost.

In Acts 26:20 Paul tells us he *"declared first to those in Damascus and in Jerusalem, and throughout all the region of Judea, and then to the Gentiles, that they should repent, turn to God, and do works befitting repentance."* It is only when one repents that one can turn to God which is affirmed by one's godliness and sinlessness.

Second Peter 3:9 reads, *"The Lord is not slack concerning His promise, as some count slackness, but is longsuffering towards us, not willing that any should perish but that all should come to repentance."*

Because God does not want anybody to go to hell, His patience with us and the numerous opportunities He gives us to repent have been taken as laxity and apathy, and hence people continue to sin.

Romans 2:4 asks: *"Or do you despise the riches of His goodness, forbearance, and longsuffering, not knowing that the goodness of God leads you to repentance?"* The patience and goodness God shows towards people are meant to give them a chance to repent.

Any perfect preaching should mention and emphasise repentance and forgiveness of sins. As we read in Luke 24:47, *"and that repentance and remission of sins should be preached in His name to all nations, beginning at Jerusalem."*

One must first repent of one's sin before one can pray to God for forgiveness of those sins. This is confirmed by Acts 8:22 which tells us, *"Repent therefore of this your wickedness, and pray God if perhaps the thought of your heart may be forgiven you."*

Conclusion

Repentance is evident when, after hearing the correct preaching of the gospel, a person acknowledges all his past sins since his childhood and expresses regret for doing them. Being sorry for his misdeeds, he now realises that it is Jesus who died to save him from his sins and who can deliver him from all his sins, and therefore turns to Him for forgiveness of all the past sins. To ensure he does not go back to his past misdeeds, he now vows and makes a covenant with Jesus not to sin anymore and this is affirmed by the Holy Spirit which is granted to him after conversion.

CHAPTER 7

BAPTISM

The subject of baptism is of vital interest to all Christians, but views and interpretations differ, especially with regard to the meaning of baptism, the modes of baptism and the subjects of baptism.

The meaning of baptism

Baptism is physical and spiritual. It is symbolic and a rite. It is administered physically, but the end result must necessarily be spiritual. Hence it is considered a sacrament in some circles; that is, an outward sign of inward grace. Baptism signifies the granting of the Holy Spirit to believers by the grace of Jesus Christ, and its efficacy depends on the spiritual status of the baptiser (the person who baptises) and the belief of the baptisee (the person being baptised) in God.

The meaning of baptism has been the subject of much controversy. Some hold the view that baptism is for the remission of sins. This view is held by numerous denominations. They support their view with passages such as, *"Repent, and let every one of you be baptised in the name of Jesus Christ for the remission of sins"* (Acts 2:38); *"Arise and be baptised, and wash away your sins"* (Acts 22:16); and *"The baptism of repentance for the remission of sins"* (Mark 1:4).

If you want to follow Christ you must repent and be baptised. To repent implies to turn from sin, changing the direction of your life from selfishness and rebellion against God's laws. At the same time, you must turn to Christ, depending on Him for forgiveness, mercy, guidance and purpose. Baptism therefore identifies us with Christ and with the community of believers; it is a condition of discipleship and a sign of faith.

A person is, therefore, converted to be baptised and not baptised to be converted. When a person is genuinely converted and he genuinely believes in God, that belief is consolidated by baptism. It is a genuine acknowledgement of sin, a genuine repentance, a genuine confession and a genuine forsaking of sin that leads to genuine conversion. When this is fulfilled then baptism can be administered, leading to the person obtaining the Holy Spirit from God.

For baptism to be real the baptiser should be a true Christian who possesses the Holy Spirit and has been sent by God, and is therefore capable of converting the baptisee. For, as it is written in Psalm 51:12-13, *"Restore to me the joy of Your salvation, and uphold me by Your generous Spirit. Then I will teach transgressors Your ways, and sinners shall be converted to You."* It is only when the baptisee is genuinely converted that he/she will have a genuine belief that qualifies him/her to be baptised.

Some oppose the view that baptism is essential to salvation (saved from eternal death). They quote Acts 16:30-31 where the jailer asks Paul and Silas what he must do to be saved. Paul and Silas replied, *"Believe on the Lord Jesus Christ, and you will be saved, you and your household."* They also quote Paul's statement in 1 Corinthians 1:14-17: *"I thank God that I baptised none of you except Crispus and Gaius, lest anyone should say that I had baptised in my own name. Yes, I also baptised the household of Stephanas. Besides, I do not know whether I baptised any other. For Christ did not send me to baptise, but to preach the gospel, not with wisdom of words, lest the cross of Christ should be made of no effect."*

Others point out that baptism is a seal of the work of grace already performed in the soul before baptism is administered, and that the subjects of baptism have already experienced regeneration and, because of this, are proper subjects for baptism. The Society of Friends (Quakers) for example, who believe in the spiritual character of Christianity, hold that the baptism of the Holy Spirit is the only prerequisite to baptism.

There are only two types of baptism, namely water baptism through John the Baptist, and Holy Spirit baptism through Jesus Christ.

In water baptism the genuine baptiser, having converted the baptisee to become a genuine believer in God, baptises with water leading to the granting of the Holy Spirit by God. The baptisee's declaration and zeal to lead a sinless life after the baptism will confirm the success of the baptism.

On the other hand, the false baptiser who himself is not born again cannot genuinely convert the baptisee and therefore the baptisee cannot have a genuine belief in God. Consequently the baptism administered by a baptiser who does not have the Holy Spirit does not lead to God granting the Holy Spirit to the baptisee. This is confirmed by there being no change in the life of the baptisee after baptism.

Water baptism which is successful leads to the granting of the Holy Spirit by God while water baptism which is a failure does not lead to the granting of the Holy Spirit and many fall into this category. Hence many people baptised by water are not born again, and continue living their old sinful nature of life.

There are many different ways of performing a water baptism, including immersion – total or partial, standing in water and pouring water over the person, aspersion – sprinkling water on the head, effusion – pouring water three times on the forehead, and others. Many churches seem to quarrel over which method is the most appropriate, but any of the methods used for water baptism may lead to the granting of Holy Spirit by God. It is not the method that matters; what matters is what leads to the granting of the Holy Spirit in water baptisms, in other words the conversion of the baptisee by the baptiser. Therefore the baptiser as well as the baptisee are determining factors of whether one gets the Holy Spirit or not.

The baptiser must have the Holy Spirit within him to convert someone, and the baptisee must be genuinely converted and genuinely believe in God. The end result of baptism is to obtain the Holy Spirit, so the type of water baptism used is immaterial. Mark 16:16 tells us, *"He who believes and is baptised will be saved; but he who does not believe will be condemned."* This confirms that without belief baptism is worthless. The belief depends on the baptiser who must be a believer, having the Holy Ghost and thus being capable of converting the baptisee into a genuine believer before baptism can be administered.

In Acts 2:38 we read, *"Then Peter said to them, 'Repent, and let every one of you be baptised in the name of Jesus Christ for the remission of sins; and you shall receive the gift of the Holy Spirit.'"* This also lays down the condition of repentance before baptism can take place.

Without genuine repentance leading to genuine conversion of the baptisee there is no need of baptism because it will not lead to the granting of the Holy Ghost by God. Acts 19:4 tells us: *"Then Paul said, 'John indeed baptised with a baptism of repentance, saying to the people that they should believe on Him who would come after him, that is, on Christ Jesus.'"* This readily affirms the importance of genuine repentance leading to a genuine belief in Jesus Christ before true baptism can be conducted.

It is stated in Galatians 3:27 that, *"For as many of you as were baptised into Christ have put on Christ."* Since the end result of baptism is the granting of the Holy Ghost by God to the baptisee, it is only if the baptisee puts on Christ by obeying God after baptism that the genuine nature of the baptism can be confirmed.

In Romans 6:4 we read *"Therefore we were buried with Him through baptism into death, that just as Christ was raised from the dead by the glory of the Father, even so we also should walk in newness of life."* This means that baptism is a dual event which shows that the old, sinful and carnal nature of the baptisee is buried with Christ on His death and on Christ's resurrection the baptisee is given a new, righteous and spiritual nature where the baptisee strives not to sin anymore.

Colossians 2:12 states, *"Buried with Him in baptism, in which you also were raised with Him through faith in the working of God, who raised Him from the dead."* This indicates that the resurrection which depicts the new nature of the baptisee goes along with faith in God, and without faith baptism is a failure.

The story of Philip and the eunuch, as it appears in Acts 8:36-40, clearly illustrates the necessity of conversion before baptism. After Philip had converted the eunuch, the man said, *"See, here is water. What hinders me from being baptised?"* And Philip said, *"If you believe with all your heart, you may."* And the eunuch answered and said, *"I believe that Jesus Christ is the son of God."* This undoubtedly is a genuine belief which would lead to the granting of the Holy Spirit by God when baptism is administered.

Ephesians 5:26 states: *"to make her holy, cleansing her by the washing with water through the word"*. As water baptism symbolises the physical washing, so the word of God symbolises spiritual washing. A true baptiser cleanses the baptisee by the word of God which he speaks to him, and with the belief of the baptisee the way is paved for the granting of the Holy Ghost by God.

Types of water baptism

The people who believe in water baptism fall into two categories: The immersionists and the non-immersionists. The immersionists dip the one being baptised into water as a sign of removal of sin. In Paul's days immersion was the usual form of baptism and new Christians were completely *"buried"* in water (Romans 6:1-4). The non-immersionists hold the view that what is essential to baptism is the application of water in the name of the Father, and of the Son, and of the Holy Spirit. This view admits any mode of baptism – pouring, sprinkling or immersion.

Holy Spirit baptism

Another form of baptism is the Holy Spirit baptism or impartation of the Holy Spirit. This is administered by the baptiser laying hands on the baptisee and the baptisee instantly receiving the Holy Ghost. It is only administered by a true Christian who has the Spirit of God living in him and who has been ordained and sent by God to baptise with the Holy Spirit. The transmission of the Holy Spirit from God is immediate and may be administered by touch, utterance, command or spiritual communication.

Just like with the water baptism, the baptisee must first be converted. The word of God preached by the baptiser to the baptisee sanctifies and cleanses the baptisee for understanding and conversion. Then the baptiser lays hands on the baptisee so they can receive the Holy Spirit.

Thearchical Domain Church practices the Holy Spirit baptism. They hold the view that at baptism all former sins are burned away, giving the baptisee the chance to lead a new life of love and obedience to God.

Examples of the Holy Spirit baptism

In Luke 1:41 we read: *"When Elizabeth heard Mary's greeting, the baby leaped in her womb, and Elizabeth was filled with the Holy Spirit."* This was the first impartation of the Holy Spirit by Jesus Christ. It was imparted to both John and Elizabeth. This was when both Jesus and John were in their mothers' wombs. Acts 8:14-17 tells us that, *"When the apostles in Jerusalem heard that Samaria had accepted the word of God, they sent Peter and John to Samaria. When they arrived, they prayed for the new believers there that they might receive the Holy Spirit, because the Holy Spirit had not yet come on any of them; they had simply been baptised in the name of the Lord Jesus. Then Peter and John placed their hands on them, and they received the Holy Spirit."*

Water baptism may or may not lead to the granting of the Holy Spirit, but Holy Spirit baptism always does because it is performed by only specially ordained priests. In Acts 19:6 we read: *"When Paul placed his hands on them, the Holy Spirit came on them, and they spoke in tongues and prophesied."* Whoever is baptised with the Holy Ghost is given at least one of the nine gifts of the Holy Spirit, but not necessarily the speaking of tongues.

In Acts 10:44 we're told: *"While Peter was still speaking these words, the Holy Spirit came on all who heard the message."* This means that Peter's preaching to the congregants converted them and they were baptised by the Holy Ghost.

The subjects of baptism

Two subjects may be identified — believers and infants.

Believers

The immersionists contend that baptism should be administered only to believers. They reject making infants the subjects of baptism on the grounds that the scriptures require that repentance and faith are essential for baptism to be administered (Acts 2:38; 8:36-37; 19:4-5). Since infants are incapable of meeting those requirements, they are not proper subjects for baptism.

Infants

With the exception of the immersionists, most protestant denominations and the Roman Catholic Church practice infant baptism. Baptists and others contend, however, that baptism should be administered only to believers. From the earliest times, though, many churches have administered it also to eight-day-old children who have sponsors to care for their Christian upbringing (Gen 17:12; Lev 12:3).

The law of heredity, set forth by Christ, states: *"That which is born of flesh is flesh"* (John 3:6). Thus the offspring of sinners can be nothing but sinners. Being by nature sinners, infants as well as adults need to be baptised. Every child that is baptised is begotten anew of water and of the spirit, is placed in covenant relation with God, and is made a child of God and an heir of His heavenly kingdom.

Conclusion

There are only two types of baptism, water baptism and spirit baptism, and both of them should lead to the consolidation of the granting of the Holy Spirit by God. For baptism to be appropriate and effective, leading to the baptisee obtaining the Holy Ghost:

The baptiser must be Holy Spirit filled and ordained by God, capable of converting the baptisee.

The baptisee must be converted by the baptiser through the word of God which cleanses and sanctifies the baptisee to have a genuine faith in God.

Baptism is an important aspect of the life of every believer. The importance of baptism is shown by the fact that the Lord Jesus Christ Himself was baptised *"to fulfil all righteousness"* (Matthew 3:15) and that He included it as part of His great commission (Matthew 28:19; Mark 16:15-16).

CHAPTER 8

HOLINESS AND RIGHTEOUSNESS

"Holy" means pure, unspotted, sinless, righteous, undefiled, sacred or saintly. Holiness is therefore saintliness, and saintliness is "sanctified in Theo" which means "made holy in God". One is made holy in God only when one is granted the Holy Spirit by God. Holiness therefore begins only when one is truly born again and therefore has the Holy Spirit living in him. It is the Holy Spirit dwelling in the person that makes the person holy. Without the Holy Spirit no one can be holy enough to exhibit holiness in their life.

"Righteous" means pure in heart, holy, upright, honest, good, moral and incorrupt. Righteousness is therefore right doing.

It is the Holy Spirit in the person that empowers him to do right, making him righteous. Holiness and righteousness go together; they are complementary. A holy person is a righteous person and a righteous person is a holy person. A holy person cannot be unrighteous and vice versa. The two are inseparable.

Holiness is the presence of righteousness, purity and goodness. It is the key to the Bible, God and heaven. The Bible is holy and is therefore called the Holy Bible, and without holiness a person cannot properly understand the Bible.

Holiness and righteousness begin the moment a person is born again. When a person is born again all their past misdeeds or sins are forgiven by God. This is when the fire precedes the Holy Spirit and burns away the past misdeeds so that the Holy Spirit can enter the body. Because the body is now a clean slate or tabula rasa, Jesus instructs "Go and sin no more", meaning "keep the holiness and righteousness henceforth", since the Holy Spirit is occupying the body. We are holy and it is this that makes the Holy Spirit bear witness with our spirit that we are children of God.

"Holiness" means God is wholly sacred; it expresses God's divine perfection. Holiness also means set apart for divine perfection.

The cross symbolises holiness and righteousness; the vertical bar signifies uprightness before God which is holiness, and the horizontal bar signifies doing right before man which is righteousness. The cross also symbolises the two commandments, being the summary of the Ten Commandments as stated in Matthew 22:37, *"Jesus said unto him, Thou shalt love the Lord your God with all your heart and with all your soul and with all your mind"* (representing holiness) and *"Love your neighbour as yourself"* (representing righteousness).

Types of holiness and righteousness

There are three types of holiness and righteousness: Physical holiness and righteousness, spiritual holiness and righteousness and then perfect holiness and righteousness which is the combination of the two.

Physical holiness and righteousness is the first era when laws had not yet been given by God. People were judged without the law by their conscience and would qualify to go to heaven paradise if they only did right and avoided doing wrong, since conscience is a person's inner awareness of conforming to the will of God, being the image of God, or departing from it due to Adamic sin.

Physical holiness and righteousness with God's law is the second era when the laws of God had been given to Moses. To go to heaven paradise one would have to keep the law in addition to keeping a clear conscience. Physical holiness and righteousness is emphasised in the Old Testament. It is the avoidance of pollution and defilement of the body which includes avoiding eating unclean meat and avoiding having contact with unclean issues out of the flesh. In Leviticus 11:44-46 God says He is holy and so his children must also be holy by not defiling themselves with unclean meat by observing the law of the beast.

The third era is the first coming of Jesus Christ when we have spiritual holiness and righteousness and there's less emphasis on the state of the body because for one to go to heaven paradise one has to accept Jesus Christ, be born again and receive the Holy Ghost. That is the only means of obtaining spiritual holiness and righteousness.

The fourth era is the second coming of Jesus Christ when we have perfect (soul or psychic) holiness and righteousness which is the combination of both physical and spiritual holiness and righteousness. This doctrine is soul doctrine and at Thearchical Domain Church sinlessness is preached and perfection reached as stated in the following passages: *"So Christ was sacrificed once to take away the sins of many; and he will appear a second time, not to bear sin, but to bring salvation to those who are waiting for him"* (Hebrews 9:28) and *"but when completeness comes, what is in part disappears"* (1 Corinthians 13:10).

Some passages on holiness and righteousness

Hebrews 12:14 reads, *"Make every effort to live in peace with everyone and to be holy; without holiness no one will see the Lord."* Holiness is a condition for one to see the Lord, and for one to be holy one must obtain the Holy Spirit.

In 1 Peter 1:15-16 we're told, *"But just as He who called you is holy, so be holy in all you do; for it is written: 'Be holy because I am holy.'"* Because Christians are supposed to be like Christ and Christ is holy, every Christian must obtain the Holy Spirit to be holy in everything they do in order to be like Jesus.

In Leviticus 11:44 and 46 God states *"I am the Lord your God; consecrate yourselves and be holy, because I am holy. Do not make yourselves unclean by any creature that moves along the ground ...This is the law of the beasts and of the fowls, and of every living creature that moveth in the waters, and of every creature that creepeth upon the earth."*

Here God teaches us that holiness also relates to the meat, the fowl and the fish that we eat. This can be termed physical or flesh holiness while the holiness through the Holy Spirit is called spiritual holiness. The physical or flesh holiness also includes avoiding blood issuing from women. For a Christian to qualify to go to soul heaven — the 6th heaven or psychic realm — one has to attain both spiritual holiness and physical holiness.

In 2 Corinthians 7:1 we read, *"Therefore, since we have these promises, dear friends, let us purify ourselves from everything that contaminates body and spirit, perfecting holiness out of reverence for God."* This affirms that perfect holiness is the combination of spiritual holiness and flesh holiness which is psychic.

Cleansing the filthiness of the flesh is the Old Testament cleansing of the body and cleansing the filthiness of the spirit is the New Testament cleansing of the spirit. For example, even if you lust after someone it's as though you have already committed the act, cautions Jesus in Matthew 5:27-28.

First Thessalonians 4:7 reminds us *"For God did not call us to be impure, but to live a holy life."* When one is called by God he is called from his uncleanness and is supposed to forsake his sins and be chosen unto holiness, but most people called by God do not forsake their sins and continue in their uncleanness and are never chosen to be holy.

Psalm 93:5 states, *"Your statutes, Lord, stand firm; holiness adorns your house for endless days."* Since God is holy his dwelling place is holiness and that is why only those having the Holy Spirit have the environment of holiness in which God can dwell.

In Genesis 18:23-33 we read about the destruction of Sodom and Gomorrah where Abraham pleaded with God to save them, and God said if He found fifty righteous people he would not destroy the cities. This number was subsequently reduced to forty-five, then forty, thirty, twenty and finally to ten, where God said if He found ten righteous people he would not destroy it. However, eventually Sodom and Gomorrah were destroyed, meaning not even ten righteous people were found.

The happenings around the world now are so appalling that it's not far-fetched to conclude that we are living in the Sodom and Gomorrah era. Evil deeds are getting worse, and indeed, if the time were not shortened those who would qualify to go to heaven would not be more than ten percent of the world's population.

"The Lord is far from the wicked, but he hears the prayer of the righteous" (Proverbs 15:29). For one's prayer to reach God the person must be righteous, meaning the person must be sinless.

In 1 John 1:7 we read, *"But if we walk in the light, as he is in the light, we have fellowship with one another, and the blood of Jesus, His Son, purifies us from all sin."* The cleansing by the blood of Jesus is spiritual cleansing which produces spiritual holiness.

John 17:17 says, *"Sanctify them by the truth; your word is truth"*, and John 15:3 tells us, *"You are already clean because of the word I have spoken to you."* The word of God itself makes us holy, provided we accept God wholly. This full acceptance of the word leads to faith which leads to the granting of the Holy Spirit by God.

Philippians 3:9 reads, *"and be found in him, not having a righteousness of my own that comes from the law, but that which is through faith in Christ – the righteousness that comes from God on the basis of faith."* This affirms the duality of righteousness. Personal righteousness which is physical is expressed by anybody for a favour done to him by others or a favour others are expecting from him. Then there's spiritual righteousness which is the righteousness after one is born again through the person's faith in God. This is expressed not for any favour done by or to be expected by the Christian, but the Holy Spirit in the Christian exhibits the inherent righteousness of Christ in him.

In Isaiah 64:6 we read *"All our righteous acts are like filthy rags"*, referring to the carnal righteousness which is of the law. In 2 Corinthians 5:21 we're reminded that *"God made Him who had no sin to be sin for us, so that in Him we might become the righteousness of God."* A Christian's righteousness is a spiritual righteousness which is the righteousness of God in Christ. In the beatitudes (Matthew 5:3-10) Jesus said *"Blessed are those who are persecuted because of righteousness."* This refers to spiritual righteousness which is present in Christians and emanates from holiness.

Second Timothy 4:8 reiterates *"Now there is in store for me the crown of righteousness, which the Lord, the righteous Judge, will award to me on that day – and not only to me, but also to all who have longed for His appearing."* This refers to spiritual righteousness which one ought to have for one to go to heaven and win a crown. The only way for one to achieve this is to be born again, that is, to receive the Holy Spirit.

Romans 10:3 mentions that *"Since they did not know the righteousness of God and sought to establish their own, they did not submit to God's righteousness."*

Any righteousness which is not of God is personal and carnal; it is demonstrated by those who have not surrendered to God and therefore are not born again.

In Romans 10:4 it is written, *"Christ is the culmination of the law so that there may be righteousness for everyone who believes."* It is only the genuine believers who have Christ's righteousness which is spiritual righteousness. Romans 10:10 emphasises that, *"it is with your heart that you believe and are justified, and it is with your mouth that you profess your faith and are saved."*

Luke 1:74-75 states: *"To rescue us from the hand of our enemies, and to enable us to serve him without fear in holiness and righteousness before him all our days."* We are delivered from our enemies only when we are born again. After this we can serve God appropriately in holiness and righteousness because we have the Holy Spirit living in us. Ephesians 4:24 reads, *"and to put on the new self, created to be like God in true righteousness and holiness."* The new man is one who's born again and therefore born of God, and with the Holy Spirit in him, he lives a holy and righteous life.

Conclusion

True holiness and true righteousness are both physical and spiritual. The two are inseparable. Spiritual holiness is obtained only through the Holy Spirit of God and the Holy Spirit is received only when a person is born again. The born again person does what is right to affirm the righteousness of Christ in him. Holy Spirit is therefore the source of holiness, and holiness leads to righteousness. The cross symbolises holiness and righteousness without which no one can enter the kingdom of God.

CHAPTER 9

WHERE CAN A PERSON GO AFTER DEATH

There are only three places available for the spirit of a dead person to go after death. Two places are available in heaven and one place is in hell. The spirit of the person is compelled to go to only one of these places according to their beliefs and life led at the time of their death. In heaven the two places are heaven paradise (also called fourth heaven) and soul heaven (also called sixth heaven or psychic realm). In hell the place is hell paradise (fourth hell). The angels of God are in the fifth heaven and the other heavens and hells are occupied by other spirits. I Corinthians 6:3 states *"Do you not know that we shall judge angels; How much more things that pertain to this life!"* It is the saints in the sixth heaven who judge the angels in the fifth heaven. Heaven is above the earth, beyond the sky, and hell is down below the surface of the earth.

Paradise

In Luke 23:43 Jesus Christ said to the criminal crucified alongside him, *"Assuredly, I say to you, today you will be with me in Paradise."* This confirms that the first coming of Jesus Christ was to take genuine believers to paradise after death.

In 2 Corinthians 12:2-4 Paul describes how his spirit was caught up to the third heaven and paradise. This paradise is the fourth heaven.

Thearc Daniel Kingsley Arthur, the founder of Thearchical Domain Church in Ghana saw God on 23 December 1952 and his spirit was taken by the Spirit of God to see hell, paradise and soul heaven. As I mentioned earlier, he described paradise as a place of moonlight, without darkness or sunlight.

He also saw Martin Luther in his balcony and Martin Luther was surprised to see Thearc emitting sunlight from his spiritual body while his was emitting moonlight.

Pastor Daniel Ekechukwu of Power Chapel Evangelical Church in Onitsha, Nigeria, who died on 30 November 2001 and was raised up from the dead after three days, also saw paradise. According to him, in paradise he saw a multitude of people all dressed in the same white apparel and with the same white body. They were singing very sweet songs and would bend and rise up simultaneously as if something was controlling them. He wanted to join them but the angel who took him there restricted him and asked Pastor Ekechukwu to follow him to the mansions which Jesus said He had built. Immediately the angel said that, they arrived at the mansions which are in soul heaven.

Soul heaven is also called the psychic realm. This is the heaven which Jesus spoke about in John 14:2-3 *"In My Father's house are many mansions; if it were not so, I would have told you. I go to prepare a place for you. And if I go and prepare a place for you, I will come again and receive you to Myself; that where I am, there you may be also."*

During the first resurrection the spiritual beings there will be upgraded and transferred to soul heaven (the sixth heaven). This is the final abode where those who die in Christ live eternally.

Soul heaven, the psychic realm or sixth heaven

The heavens and the things in them are just as material as those on earth. Invisible things are made up of material substance which is visible in its own realm. In our physical mortal body on earth we live in mansions according to our status, and in the same way in our spiritual immortal body in heaven we'll live in varying mansions according to the level of crown we deserve. The mansions are where all the saints will live eternally, hence it is called world without end.

This is the heaven that Jesus spoke about in Matthew 11:11 *"Assuredly, I say to you, among those born of women there has not risen one greater than John the Baptist; but he who is least in the kingdom of heaven is greater than he."* The kingdom of heaven is the sixth heaven where John the Baptist and the other saints in heaven paradise, the fourth heaven, go during the first resurrection.

Description of soul heaven

Thearc (the teacher of saints) Daniel Arthur, whose spirit was taken to see soul heaven, describes it as follows in his book "Mystical Experience": "With two mystical steps upwards with the spirit, we reached a calm and bright location. Indeed the place was exceedingly beautiful with two large corridors. One stretched from north to south and the other corridor stretched from east to the west. Even the floor of the corridors was covered with velvety cushion carpet, shiny and comfortable such as fills the heart with deepest sensation of untold bliss. There I saw human beings with transparent bodies and in glorious sheen each sitting comfortably by the wide table measuring about four and a half feet by two and a half feet.

"I walked towards the east of the velvety cushion floor, and while proceeding I saw one of the transparent bodies standing up and looking at me in amazement. He made a signal and all of them stood up in obeisance. As they stood up, they realised that I had obtained the same transparent body with different blood and colour. But I towered above them in height. The Spirit then told me that I was in the psychic realm or sixth heaven and that the respectful homage they paid to me meant that they were astonished to see a man reaching the psychic realm direct from earth. I noticed also that activities in the sixth heaven are sublime. They travel miles away by just rising up from their seats without moving a step. They communicate without words but made signals with their fingers.

"As I walked through the city there appeared above me a very bright orb. Within it was a sparkling circling object like a barbed wire.

"The glittering object threw a very powerful beam over me. The light, incomparable to any earthly searchlight, shined through my transparent body. I felt rather cold, yet the rays of that light were as bright as the sun. That event, I was made to understand, was a fiery initiation of the Holy Spirit, to purge the stains of my parental sins in preparation for meeting Jehovah — the king of all creation. Suddenly I found myself on my bed with my heart beating very fast, my body shaking and looking terribly afraid, but I was filled with immense joy for that delightful mystical adventure."

According to Pastor Ekechukwu, when he was in soul heaven he saw indescribably beautiful mansions. He also saw that the whole place was paved with gold and there were even gold flowers. Then the angel told him, "Jesus says He has finished with the mansions but the saints are not ready."

Does the angel's utterance mean that the apostles of Jesus and those who died in the Lord are not saints? No. All of them are second-class saints who are in paradise. They will leave paradise for the psychic realm to become first-class saints during the first resurrection of the dead when their physical bodies on earth will join their spiritual bodies, spirit and soul, to live eternally.

Jesus' first coming by the Spirit took true believers to spirit heaven, which is paradise.

In John 14:12 Jesus said *"Most assuredly, I say to you, he who believes in Me, the works that I do he will do also; and greater works than these he will do, because I go to My Father."* This confirms the greater work Jesus would do after his second coming.

In Hebrews 9:28 we read *"So Christ was offered once to bear the sins of many. To those who eagerly wait for Him He will appear a second time, apart from sin, for salvation."*

Whenever a person dies many sympathizers express their condolences by saying, "May his/her soul rest in peace." Unfortunately many people who die do not even have an immortal soul for it to rest in peace in soul heaven.

Psalm 23:3 states, *"He restores my soul: he leads me in the paths of righteousness for His name's sake."* It was the soul which was the power of God, the Holy Spirit that Adam and Eve lost when they sinned in the Garden of Eden. Consequently anybody born into the world does not have an immortal soul and it has to be restored. The soul is restored only when the Holy Spirit of God is received. It is therefore only the true Christians whose real souls have been restored. All others have mortal souls without the Holy Spirit.

Hell paradise and the hell lake of fire

Hell paradise is the fourth hell. It is a place of unbearable torment with unquenchable fire in the spirit body. Thearc Daniel Kingsley Arthur described his visit to hell as follows: "I had to embark upon fervent prayers, fasting and meditations in a quest for wisdom and understanding. After many years with the zeal, by prayers, fasting and meditations, I was one day forced into psycroscopic subtility, a state which is termed 'panorama'. There I saw the inexhaustible riches of the celestial world with living rays that marvel all those accosted unto the level of the serene zone. In that panoramic state my spirit was awakened by another spirit which took one mystical step downward with me. We reached a place that was very dark and overcrowded with people all standing. The overcrowding was such that one stepping upon another's foot did not apologise. The expressions on their faces showed that they were in agony. The spirit named that place as hell and, being in a gnostic state, I got to know that it was hell paradise."

Pastor Daniel Ekechukwu's experience in hell

After the angel had taken Pastor Daniel Ekechukwu to soul heaven, the angel then told him they were going to hell. As soon as the angel said that they were at the gate of hell and saw a very bold inscription: "Welcome to the gate of hell". The angel waved his hand up and down and the gate opened with a loud noise. He saw overcrowded people wearing the clothes in which they'd died; they could be identified by their race (white, Indian, Asian, black etc.) unlike what he'd seen in paradise.

The place was dark, and he could only see his way through by the light surrounding the angel. Pastor Ekechukwu said they were wailing and crying aloud and although he did not see any fire there, it appeared something like fire was burning them from the way they reacted. One of them shouted "I am a pastor and I only stole church money and I am brought here, and I am prepared to pay." That one directed his speech to Pastor Ekechukwu as if he did not see the angel standing alongside him.

Before they moved on from that place the angel told Pastor Ekechukwu that he too was headed for hell. Pastor Ekechukwu argued that he was a pastor and did not belong in hell. However the angel reminded him that on the morning of his death his wife offended him and asked for forgiveness but he did not forgive her, so that alone would have landed him in hell. The angel again reminded him that while he was on his death bed Pastor Ekechukwu prayed to God for forgiveness but God did not forgive him before he died because he had not forgiven his wife. Then Pastor Ekechukwu wept. The angel told him not to weep because God was going to use him to fulfil the request that the rich man in the Bible made when he asked God to send someone to the earth to tell his five siblings to change so that they would not go to hell where he was.

Then the angel led Pastor Ekechukwu to a high mountain where they could see a big dark hole and a man standing there who the pastor could not identify at first. When they got closer he saw that the man was his head pastor Reinhard Bonnke, then his eyes moved to the table where his own body lay in state at the church.

Conclusion

There are only three places available for the deceased to choose from after death. The choice depends on their belief and the life they lived prior to passing away. The three places available are heaven paradise, soul heaven and hell paradise as described above. If people would only believe in the reality of hell, and that any deliberate sin – be it one or more – would lead one to hell, nobody on earth would sin. The choice is yours, but be reminded and do not be deceived by any contrary doctrine – any sin, be it one or more, committed up to the time of death will certainly take a person to hell.

CHAPTER 10

HOW CAN I GO TO HEAVEN?

Heaven is real, and whoever is called or called and chosen by God believes that, because the Bible says so, and therefore wishes to go there. Indeed, many, many, many people are called, but very, very, very few are chosen among the called to become God's children.

Many who are called and not chosen are those sitting between two stools – they are neither hot nor cold. Jesus says in Revelation 3:16 *"So then, because you are lukewarm, and neither cold nor hot, I will vomit you out of My mouth."* These people try to please God and the world. They serve God and mammon, as the word of God says; consequently they are in doubt – unsure of going to heaven because they do not obey God absolutely.

The very few who are called and chosen are one hundred percent sure of going to heaven when they die because they live a sinless life and obey God absolutely. This is affirmed by Romans 8:16 which says, *"The Spirit Himself bears witness with our spirit, that we are the children of God."* For it is only the children of God who obey God absolutely and thus qualify to go to heaven.

To go to heaven you must of necessity be sinless. This sinlessness is possible only when the Holy Spirit dwells in you and controls you so that you cannot intentionally commit sin.

The procedure to follow to go to heaven is simply this:

- Be a full member of a church where you can be born again.

- Receive the Holy Spirit as a confirmation of you being born again.

- Do not deliberately sin again, as an affirmation of having received the Holy Spirit since the Holy Spirit gives you power to refrain from sin.

- Continue to live a sinless life in this world until God calls you into his heavenly kingdom either in paradise, the fourth heaven, or in soul heaven also called the psychic realm or the sixth heaven.

The following passages from the Bible, quoting Jesus speaking about the importance of being *"born again"*, will further explain how you can go to heaven:

- *"Most assuredly, I say to you, unless one is born again, he cannot see the kingdom of God."* (John 3:3)

- *"Most assuredly, I say to you, unless one is born of water and the Spirit, he cannot enter the kingdom of God."* (John 3:5)

- *"That which is born of the flesh is flesh; and that which is born of the Spirit is spirit."* (John 3:6)

These three statements show that for a person to enter into the kingdom of God that person must of necessity be born again and that birth must be spiritual where the Holy Spirit is given to the person and they are now born of God.

How can one be born again?

First and foremost one must be in a church where one can be born again and receive the Holy Spirit. Romans 10:13-15 states, *"Whoever calls on the name of the Lord shall be saved. How then shall they call on Him in whom they have not believed? And how shall they believe in Him of whom they have not heard? And how shall they hear without a preacher? And how shall they preach unless they are sent?"*

The most serious problem with the church is that most of the preachers have not been sent by God and therefore they do not qualify to preach and their preaching is such that it cannot lead to repentance and conversion of the congregation. When a congregant hears the preaching of the preacher sent by God, he repents of his sins, believes in Jesus Christ and is converted. He is then baptised to receive the Holy Spirit that will enable him to live a sinless life and eventually go to heaven.

Living according to the following passages will confirm that one is sinless and indeed able to go to heaven.

- *"Whoever abides in Him does not sin. Whoever sins has neither seen Him nor known Him."* (1 John 3:6)

- *"Whoever has been born of God does not sin, for His seed remains in him; and he cannot sin, because he has been born of God."* (1 John 3:9)

- *"We know that whoever is born of God does not sin; but he who has been born of God keeps himself, and the wicked one does not touch him."* (1 John 5:18)

- *"Now he who keeps His commandments abides in Him, and He in him. And by this we know that He abides in us, by the Spirit whom He has given us."* (1 John 3:24)

- *"But be doers of the word, and not hearers only, deceiving yourselves."* (James 1:22)

- *"The devising of foolishness is sin."* (Proverbs 24:9)

- *"Any unrighteousness is sin."* (1 John 5:17)

In Matthew 7:21 Jesus again said, *"Not everyone who says to Me, 'Lord, Lord,' shall enter the kingdom of heaven, but he who does the will of My Father in heaven."* This affirms how Jesus is very aware that many people praise God, worship God and pray to God with the hope of going to heaven, but he warns that only those who do the will of the Father (those who obey God and are therefore without sin) will qualify to go to heaven.

James 2:10-11 tells us, *"For whoever shall keep the whole law, and yet stumble in one point, he is guilty of all. For He who said 'Do not commit adultery' also said 'Do not murder'. Now if you do not commit adultery but you do murder, you have become a transgressor of the law."* This reiterates that a person must not commit even one sin if they want to go to heaven.

In Matthew 18:3 Jesus said, *"Assuredly, I say to you, unless you are converted and become as little children, you will by no means enter the kingdom of heaven."* Jesus is again emphasising that for a person to enter into the kingdom of God it is imperative that the person changes from the old carnal nature of sin to the new spiritual nature without sin, just as little children are sinless and therefore qualify to go to heaven.

1 Corinthians 6:9-11 states, *"Do you not know that the unrighteous will not inherit the kingdom of God? Do not be deceived. Neither fornicators, nor idolaters, nor adulterers, nor homosexuals, nor sodomites, nor thieves, nor covetous, nor drunkards, nor revilers, nor extortioners will inherit the kingdom of God. And such were some of you. But you were washed, but you were sanctified, but you were justified in the name of the Lord Jesus and by the Spirit of our God."* This passage teaches us that anybody who continues to knowingly do any wrong thing does not qualify to go to heaven. A few wrong doings have been cited here as examples, but the list of wrong doings is much, much longer.

In short, any one sin which you do disqualifies you from going to heaven. People who do wrong things and still hope to get into heaven are deceiving themselves. The passage continues to say the born again Christian was once unrighteous, doing wrong things, but now that he is born again he has stopped doing any wrong thing and does only right things because of the Holy Spirit living in him. He now qualifies to go to heaven.

Deuteronomy 26:15 tells us that heaven is the dwelling place of God *"Look down from Your holy habitation, from heaven, and bless Your people Israel and the land which You have given us, just as You swore to our fathers, 'a land flowing with milk and honey'."* According to Isaiah 66:1-2, *"Thus says the Lord: 'Heaven is My throne, And earth is My footstool.'"* Heaven is a holy habitation because of God's presence. People therefore direct their prayers to heaven, acknowledging at the same time that God is everywhere.

Psalm 24:3 asks *"Who may ascend into the hill of the Lord? Or who may stand in His holy place?"* To go to heaven is to be God's guest, but one must be qualified to come into the presence of God. David answers that question in Psalm 15:2 *"He who walks uprightly, And works righteousness, And speaks the truth in his heart."* God requires anyone seeking company with Him to have personal purity (holiness) and interpersonal integrity (righteousness); that is, they must conform to His ethical and moral standards.

Micah 6:8 tells us, *"He has shown you, O man, what is good; And what does the Lord require of you But to do justly, To love mercy, And to walk humbly with your God?"*

God is God and man is man. As such there is an infinite gap between the highest in man and the lowest in God. This gap is impossible to bridge from man's side, so if the gap is to be bridged it must be from God's side. That means that somehow we must be made holy – just as holy as God is. Any holiness which falls short of God's holiness will not be able to stand in the presence of God. Therefore, because of the holiness of God, we must have a new life in which our sins have been forgiven and done away with so that we actually can be as separated from our sin as God is. Christ has done this for us.

This is the good news of the gospel — that Christ died for our sins, having taken them upon Himself, and has set us apart from them. Because of what Jesus has done we can enter boldly into the presence of God. The only requirement then, is to believe in Christ for God to treat us as though we were as righteous as Christ. 2 Corinthians 5:21 says, *"For He made Him who knew no sin to be sin for us, that we might become the righteousness of God in Him."* The Bible calls this type of righteousness *"imputed righteousness"*. (See Romans 4:6.) That simply means that God credits to our spiritual account the very worth of Christ, as though He were a banker adding an inexhaustible deposit to our bank account.

The Bible clearly urges all men to trust in Jesus Christ as saviour and thus be reckoned as righteous by God. (See Romans 4:24.) This is the only way we can go to heaven. No man, by himself, can qualify to go to heaven; the requirements are too onerous. Hence the Lord's offer in John 14:6 where Jesus tells his disciple Thomas, *"I am the way, the truth, and the life. No one comes to the Father except through Me."*

Conclusion

For you to go to heaven you must be born again, confirmed by the Holy Spirit living in you, which is affirmed by the sinless life you lead continuously until the end when God calls you into his heavenly kingdom. That may be either in paradise, also called the fourth heaven, or in soul heaven which is also called the psychic realm or sixth heaven.

CHAPTER 11

FORNICATION

Fornication is any sexual relationship outside marriage, whether the person is married or not. Adultery (a form of fornication) is a sexual relationship between a married man and someone other than his wife, or a sexual relationship between a married woman and someone other than her husband.

Fornication includes pre-marital sex, adultery, prostitution, homosexuality, incest and bestiality. (See Leviticus 18:23.) Fornication is also used symbolically in scripture to mean following after idols as a form of abandoning God. (See Revelation 14:8 and 17:4.)

Sexual fornication is the most serious among all pardonable sins and yet it is one of the most common sins in the world. It is the sin which resists and prevents the Holy Spirit from entering the body of a nominal Christian and drives away or expels the Holy Spirit in a true Christian even before the Christian commits it, because the Holy Spirit cannot stay and be polluted.

This is the sin that David committed against the Holy Spirit which had been dwelling in him; hence he wrote in Psalm 51:11 *"Do not cast me away from Your presence, And do not take Your Holy Spirit from me."* Because David genuinely repented of his sin, the Holy Spirit was given to him again as he pleaded in Psalm 51:12 *"Restore to me the joy of Your salvation, And uphold me by Your generous Spirit."*

The Spirit taught Thearc Daniel the psychic interpretation of the tree of the knowledge of good and evil which Adam and Eve ate from, and he shared it as follows: It was Satan who danced to arouse the sexual instinct of Eve that made her persuade Adam to have pre-marital sex. They fornicated. It was not yet time for them to come together as husband and wife, hence they sinned through fornication. Consequently they lost the soul, the Spirit of God in them, and they died spiritually. God had already warned Adam that if they ate the fruit of the tree of the knowledge of good and evil they would surely die. Hence it is through fornication that sin came into the world.

The seriousness of the sin of fornication

"Foods for the stomach and the stomach for foods, but God will destroy both it and them. Now the body is not for sexual immorality but for the Lord, and the Lord for the body." (1 Corinthians 6:13) God and fornication are incompatible – diametrically opposed – since the body is for the Lord and the Lord for the body, but the Lord is always holy so that means the body must also be holy. Since the body is not for fornication, it follows that fornication is unholiness; whoever fornicates therefore does not have the Holy Spirit and therefore is not a Christian.

"For this is the will of God, your sanctification: that you should abstain from sexual immorality." (1 Thessalonians 4:3) The wish of God is that everybody becomes holy, and to achieve this one must stop fornication which is unholiness; hence whoever fornicates is not a Christian because he does not have the Holy Spirit in him.

"Flee sexual immorality. Every sin that a man does is outside the body, but he who commits sexual immorality sins against his own body." (1 Corinthians 6:18) Every other sin committed is outside the body, but fornication which is unholiness is the only one which is committed within the body and thus has the greatest control over the body, hence whoever fornicates does not have the Holy Spirit in him.

"Do you not know that your bodies are members of Christ? Shall I then take the members of Christ and make them members of a harlot? Certainly not!" (1 Corinthians 6:15) The body of any true Christian is holy because Christ lives in it. A Christian should never use his body for fornication because then he will lose Christ. Anyone who continues to fornicate is a harlot.

"Nevertheless, because of sexual immorality, let each man have his own wife, and let each woman have her own husband." (1 Corinthians 7:2) Since it is impossible for one to be a Christian as long as one commits fornication, each person must have their own wife or husband in order not to fornicate. Sadly some people who go to church and are married still commit adultery which is a form of fornication.

"But I say to you that whoever divorces his wife for any reason except sexual immorality causes her to commit adultery; and whoever marries a woman who is divorced commits adultery." (Matthew 5:32) Since fornication is the only sin that allows for divorce to take place, it shows the seriousness of fornication and why a Christian should avoid it.

Physical and spiritual fornication

Jesus stated in Matthew 5:28: *"But I say to you that whoever looks at a woman to lust for her has already committed adultery with her in his heart."* This is spiritual fornication which does not include any physical action. Physical fornication is both spiritual fornication and physical action; both of them are serious.

Conclusion

Fornication is a sexual relationship which is the most serious sin in the body and spirit. It is a sin that resists and prevents the Holy Spirit from entering any person who commits it.

If a true Christian who possesses the Holy Spirit lusts to commit physical fornication, the Holy Spirit leaves the body before the fornication takes place to avoid being polluted.

It is a sin that a Christian dare not commit because then he may lose the Holy Spirit which he may not get again, and even if the Holy Spirit is restored, a Christian will never obtain the crown in heaven which he would have obtained if he had not lost it.

CHAPTER 12

DEATH

Death is loss of life. It is lifelessness – the opposite of life. Without life there cannot be death, and therefore for one to understand death one must first understand life and its origin.

Genesis 2:7 states that, *"The Lord God formed man of the dust of the ground, and breathed into his nostrils the breath of life; and man became a living being."*

When God formed man of the dust, Adam could not move or talk, but when God breathed the breath of life into his nostrils he became a living soul. God is the only source of life. The life God gave to Adam was both spiritual and physical. There are two types of spirit – the supernatural spirit which is the soul and part of God in man which is the Holy Spirit, and the ordinary spirit which is lifeless.

It is the supernatural spirit called the soul which Adam and Eve lost when they sinned. God had warned Adam and Eve thus: *"but of the tree of the knowledge of good and evil you shall not eat, for in the day that you eat of it you shall surely die"* (Genesis 2:17). God meant firstly the immediate spiritual death caused by the sin they committed which led to the loss of the soul. When they sinned they did not immediately die physically, but continued to live for a long time, confirming that their sin led to spiritual death. The physical death followed later on.

As a result of Adam's sin that led to spiritual death, everybody born into the world bears the sin and is therefore spiritually dead. This is confirmed in Psalm 51:5 which reads, *"Behold, I was brought forth in iniquity, and in sin my mother conceived me."*

Everybody born into the world is therefore spiritually dead until their soul is restored by being born again of God when they receive the Holy Spirit. People continue to be alive without the soul, just having the ordinary spirit and the blood which is physical life. Spiritual death is separation from God because of sin.

The next type of death is physical death; this is when the body and the spirit are separated. As the origin of man was integration of the spiritual and the physical to have life, so the disintegration of the spiritual and the physical means the separation of the spirit and the body which leads to physical death. This is a universal death which everybody born into the world will have to undergo.

After the physical death the spirits and souls of those who die in the Lord Jesus Christ go to either heaven paradise (fourth heaven) or soul heaven (sixth heaven or psychic realm). In the first resurrection those in paradise will go to the soul heaven and live there eternally.

Those who die physically without the Lord go to hell paradise which is the fourth hell. They remain there until the second resurrection when they are sent to the seventh hell which is the lake of fire where they will suffer eternally. This is the second death and eternal death which is eternal separation from God because one chooses to remain separated from God in sin. Hence there are three types of death – physical death, spiritual death and eternal death.

Since it is sin that leads to death, when one is born again and no longer sins deliberately, one avoids spiritual death and eternal death and the only death a Christian has to experience is the physical death. On the other hand, whoever is not born again and therefore continues to sin undergoes all the three types of death.

Scriptural passages on death

God forewarned Adam thus: *"But of the tree of the knowledge of good and evil you shall not eat, for in the day that you eat of it you shall surely die."* (Genesis 2:17) God did not mince His words but emphasised that sin leads directly to death, and without sin there would be no death.

Romans 6:23 tells us: *"For the wages of sin is death, but the gift of God is eternal life in Christ Jesus our Lord."* This reiterates that it is sin that leads to death, so to avoid eternal death it is imperative that a person stops sinning. The reward from God for those who do not sin is eternal life.

Romans 5:12 reads: *"Therefore, just as through one man sin entered the world, and death through sin, and thus death spread to all men, because all sinned."* Sin came into the world through Adam and death came into the world because of sin, just as God had warned Adam. Consequently Adamic sin and death are passed on to anybody born into the world. If Adam had not sinned, there would not be sin or death in the world. It is for this reason that Christ came into the world – to save mankind. Since Christ indeed conquered Satan, sin and death, whoever genuinely accepts Christ stops sinning and avoids spiritual and eternal death, gaining everlasting life in heaven.

Proverbs 14:32 reminds us, *"But the righteous has a refuge in his death."* It is only the righteous, those who obey God by doing what is right, that will escape the eternal death. Any true Christian is righteous and has the assurance of a place in heaven.

Psalm 116:15 affirms that, *"Precious in the sight of the Lord is the death of His saints."* Saint means "sanctified in Theo" or "made holy in God". Holiness and righteousness go together. It is only a true Christian who is both holy and righteous and his death means a lot to God; by being faithful to God unto the end he will gain the crown of life.

"For to me, to live is Christ, and to die is gain" (Philippians 1:21). Christ is everything to a true Christian because a Christian depends wholly on Christ and therefore cannot live without Him. To die is gain to a Christian because he is certain of going to be with the Lord in heaven for an everlasting joy and happiness where there is no pain, no disease, no sickness and no want.

In Revelation 14:13 we're told: *"Then I heard a voice from heaven saying to me, 'Write: "Blessed are the dead who die in the Lord from now on." Yes,' says the Spirit, 'that they may rest from their labours, and their works follow them.'"* Those who die in the Lord are those Christians who are sinless at the point of death; it is their faithfulness and obedience to God that will follow them in the end. They are blessed because their destination is heaven where there is everlasting bliss and rest.

Hebrews 9:27 warns *"and as it is appointed for men to die once, but after this the judgment"*. This is a warning to everybody that death is bound to come and it is judgment that follows where one is either set free to go to heaven and enjoy perfect bliss, or be proved guilty and suffer eternal torment and damnation.

Romans 3:23 acknowledges that, *"All have sinned and fall short of the glory of God."* Since the wages of sin is death, it means all people have sinned and do not meet the expectation of God which is sinlessness. Hence Jesus Christ came to overcome Satan and sin and death so that whosoever genuinely accepts Jesus Christ also overcomes Satan, sin and death. The genuineness of the acceptance is only affirmed by the sinless life exhibited by a truly born again Christian.

In John 11:25-26 Jesus said to Martha, *"I am the resurrection and the life. He who believes in Me, though he may die, he shall live. And whoever lives and believes in Me shall never die. Do you believe this?"* Here Jesus emphasises the importance of belief in order to overcome death and have everlasting life. It is only a Christian who lives a sinless life who genuinely believes in Christ because one cannot claim to believe in Christ if one continues to sin.

Romans 8:6 tells us that *"To be carnally minded is death, but to be spiritually minded is life and peace."* Any true Christian has the Holy Spirit living in him and therefore has the mind of the Holy Spirit. As stated in 1 Corinthians 2:16 *"For 'Who has known the mind of the Lord that he may instruct Him?' But we have the mind of Christ."* Every true Christian therefore has the mind of Christ and has life and peace. Any person who continues in sin has a sinful mind and therefore eternal death is his end.

The first death

The first death is the universal death for any person who ever lived. It is the separation of the body from the spirit. In the first death, those who were saved and died in the Lord are taken to heaven paradise or soul heaven, but those who were unsaved and did not die in the Lord are taken to hell paradise. During the first resurrection, the bodies of those who died in the Lord will join their spirits and souls in paradise and soul heaven and all of them will live together eternally in soul heaven.

The second death

The second death is only for those who are unsaved and who are in hell paradise. It occurs during the second resurrection when all the unsaved and forsaken beings in hell paradise will be taken to the lake of fire as affirmed by the following passages:

- *"Then Death and Hades were cast into the lake of fire. This is the second death."* (Revelation 20:14)
- *"And anyone not found written in the Book of Life was cast into the lake of fire."* (Revelation 20:15)
- *"But the cowardly, unbelieving, abominable, murderers, sexually immoral, sorcerers, idolaters, and all liars shall have their part in the lake which burns with fire and brimstone, which is the second death."* (Revelation 21:8)

Conclusion

Apart from Jesus Christ and John the Baptist who were born with the Holy Spirit, whoever is born in the world does not come with the Holy Spirit and therefore is spiritually dead though physically alive, because of Adamic sin. When a person is born again and receives the Holy Spirit, the person becomes spiritually alive. When a born again person dies physically there is a physical and spiritual separation where the physical sleeps and the spiritual lives eternally. The soul which is restored when a person is born again goes back to God, but the body is resurrected during the first resurrection. At the physical death of the unsaved there is also a physical and spiritual separation, but because the soul was not restored the spiritual death is eternal and the body is resurrected during the second resurrection.

CHAPTER 13

WHO IS GOD?

God is the source and origin of the universe, both material and immaterial. God is a supreme spiritual being who was neither created nor born. There is none above Him and none below Him. He created everything in the universe, the heavens and the earth. He is a male because He describes Himself as a Father and as being three in one; Father, Son and Holy Spirit. Since He is the Alpha and Omega, the beginning and the end of everything, for one to understand Him and His creation, one must love and wholly understand the written word about Him- the Bible.

The nature of God

"God is Spirit, and those who worship Him must worship in spirit and truth." (John 4:24). Since God is spirit, for one to worship Him in spirit and in truth, one must have God's spirit in him, just as for one to see Him one must have a pure heart with the Spirit of God in him.

God is omnipotent

God is all-powerful. *"And when Abram was 90 years old and nine, the Lord appeared to Abram and said unto Him; 'I am Almighty God; walk before Me and be blameless.'"* (Genesis 17:1)

God is omnipresent

God is always present; He is everywhere. *"Where can I go from Your Spirit? Or where can I flee from Your presence? If I ascend into heaven, You are there; If I make my bed in hell, behold, You are there. If I take the wings of the morning, And dwell in the uttermost parts of the sea, Even there Your hand shall lead me,*

And Your right hand shall hold me. If I say, 'Surely the darkness shall fall on me,' Even the night shall be light about me Indeed, the darkness shall not hide from You, But the night shines as the day; The darkness and the light are both alike to You." (Psalm 139:7-12)

God is omniscient

God is all knowing. "Oh, the depth of the riches both of the wisdom and knowledge of God! How unsearchable are His judgments and His ways past finding out!" (Romans 11:33)

God is changeless

God does not change. "Like a cloak You will fold them up, And they will be changed. But you are the same, And Your years will not fail." (Hebrew 1:12)

God is eternal

"Before the mountains were brought forth, or ever you had formed the earth and the world, even from everlasting to everlasting, you are God." (Psalm 90:2)

God is the Trinity

God is three persons – Father, Son and Holy Ghost.

"For there are three that bear witness in heaven, the Father, the Word, and the Holy Ghost; and these three are one." (1 John 5:7 NKJV)

God is holy

Holy comes from a root word that means *"to separate"*. It refers to God as separated from or exalted above other things. *"And one cried onto another and said 'Holy, Holy, Holy is the Lord of hosts, the whole earth is full of his glory.'"* (Isaiah 6:3) Holiness refers to God's moral excellence. Holiness is God's gift that we receive by faith through His Son Jesus Christ. (Ephesians 4:24) Holiness is the absence of faults. It means to be cleared of faults and set apart by God. It is purity.

God is righteous

God is good, upright and virtuous. The righteousness of God refers to His moral laws laid down to guide the conduct of mankind.

God is love

God gave His Son to suffer for mankind. Love must be evident between God and man, between neighbours and between husband and wife. There are different kinds of love — agape, divine love, neighbourly, brotherly love. God's love is agape and divine humble love.

God is truth

God is absolute truth for it is impossible for God to lie.

God is wisdom

He is the only wise God. *"Now to the King eternal, immortal, invisible, to God who alone is wise, be honour and glory forever and ever. Amen."* (1 Timothy 1:17)

God is forgiving

"To the Lord our God belong mercy and forgiveness, though we have rebelled against Him." (Daniel 9:9)

God has a soul

"God said, 'I will set My tabernacle among you, and My soul shall not abhor you I will walk among you and be your God, and you shall be My people.'" (Leviticus 26:11-12)

"Yes, I will rejoice over them to do them good, and I will assuredly plant them in this land, with all My heart and with all My soul." (Jeremiah 32:41)

Since God was not made or created by anyone, no one is greater than Him. Hence He is supreme and almighty. He is the source of life and creator of all things as stated in John 1:3. He never changes as we do. He never grows older or weaker. He has no beginning and no end. He is the same yesterday, today and forever. We are conditioned by a lifespan of about 80 years but God is not limited by time. He always existed and will forever exist.

God and Jesus were together in the beginning as stated in John 1:1 *"In the beginning was the Word, and the Word was with God, and the Word was God."*

Colossians 1:16 tells us, *"For by Him all things were created that are in heaven and that are on earth, visible and invisible, whether thrones or dominions or principalities or powers. All things were created through Him and for Him."*

The fruits of the spirit are the attributes of God, these are *"love, joy, peace, longsuffering, kindness, goodness, faithfulness, gentleness, self-control."* (Galatians 5:22-23)

Conclusion

God is God. He is almighty and supreme; His power is infinite and everything about Him is beyond human understanding.

CHAPTER 14

WHO IS JESUS CHRIST?

Jesus Christ has three names which define him. Christ means the anointed one (Messiah), Jesus means the saviour, and Emmanuel means God with us. When we combine the three names we see that Jesus Christ is the anointed one who has come to save us and be with us forever.

Jesus Christ is both divine and human. As a divine being He is a supreme being and yet he is human with the nature of man – frail and subject to sin. Jesus Christ is the Son of God and the Son of Man. He also has a soul, as He stated in Matthew 26:38, *"Then He said to them, 'My soul is exceedingly sorrowful, even to death. Stay here and watch with me.'"*

Jesus Christ and God the Father

Jesus Christ has been with the Father from the beginning. As we read in John 1:1 *"In the beginning was the Word, and the Word was with God, and the Word was God."* Jesus Christ is God. Jesus Christ is therefore the Word, hence the Holy Bible from Genesis to Revelation is Jesus Christ in words. Because Jesus Christ is God, He has all the attributes of God the Father – both the natural and moral attributes. Jesus and the Father are one, but the Father is greater than the Son. All power on earth and in heaven has been given Him by the Father. The Father spared Him to come to the earth to die and shed His blood on earth to bring reconciliation between the Father and man because the Adamic sin had separated man from Him and only the shedding of blood could pacify God and ensure the forgiveness of man's sins.

The mission of Jesus Christ on Earth

Jesus came into the world to conquer Satan, save us from sin and reconcile man to God, for man who was created in the image of God had sinned and therefore was separated from God his creator. Sin is the only thing that separates man from God and sin is caused by Satan. Jesus' mission was to conquer Satan and save us from sin so that whoever accepts Christ conquers Satan and therefore conquers sin.

In Genesis 2:17 we read that God forewarned Adam about sin: *"but of the tree of the knowledge of good and evil you shall not eat, for in the day that you eat of it you shall surely die."* So when Adam and Eve sinned they lost the Spirit of God in them and they died spiritually; they became dead souls and without the soul they now lived with a lifeless spirit. Christ came to the earth to restore the lost soul to man; hence it is written is Psalm 23:3 *"He restores my soul."* It is only when a person is born again that the soul is restored as the Holy Spirit is given to the person.

When a person is born again both the Adamic sin and the sins committed by the person since birth are taken away and the person is now reconciled to God by the Spirit of God being granted to the person. Jesus Christ warns born-again Christians not to sin anymore lest they lose the Holy Spirit.

Passages to confirm the mission of Jesus

- *"And she will bring forth a Son, and you shall call His name Jesus, for He will save His people from their sins."* (Matthew 1:21)

- *"For I delivered to you first of all that which I also received: that Christ died for our sins according to the Scriptures."* (1 Corinthians 15:3)

- *"He who sins is of the devil, for the devil has sinned from the beginning. For this purpose the Son of God was manifested, that He might destroy the works of the devil."* (1 John 3:8)

- *"The thief does not come except to steal, and to kill, and to destroy. I have come that they may have life, and that they may have it more abundantly."* (John 10:10)

- *"For through Him we both have access by one Spirit to the Father."* (Ephesians 2:18)

- *"For the Son of Man is come to seek and to save that which was lost."* (Luke 19:10)

- *"For God did not send His Son into the world to condemn the world, but that the world through Him might be saved."* (John 3:17)

- *"This is a faithful saying and worthy of all acceptance, that Christ Jesus came into the world to save sinners, of whom I am chief."* (1 Timothy 1:15)

- *"But is now made manifest by the appearing of our saviour Jesus Christ who hath abolished death, and that brought life and immortality to light through the gospel."* (2 Timothy 1:10)

Jesus and Adam

"And so it is written, 'The first man Adam became a living being.' The last Adam became a life-giving spirit." (1 Corinthians 15:45)

"However, the spiritual is not first, but the natural, and afterward the spiritual." (1 Corinthians 15:46)

"The first man was of the earth, made of dust; the second Man is the Lord from heaven." (1 Corinthians 15:47)

"But now Christ is risen from the dead, and has become the first fruits of those who have fallen asleep." (1 Corinthians 15:20)

"For since by man came death, by Man also came the resurrection of the dead." (1 Corinthians 15:21)

"For as in Adam all die, even so in Christ all shall be made alive." (1 Corinthians 15:22)

The first coming of Jesus Christ

Jesus' first coming to the earth was to take people who believed in Him to heaven paradise as he rightly assured the criminal on the cross: *"And Jesus said to him, 'Assuredly, I say to you, today you will be with Me in Paradise'"* (Luke 23:43). Paradise is the fourth heaven where people who died in Christ go after death. This means at the point of death one is already born again, filled with the Holy Spirit and is sinless.

In Paul's vision which he relates in 2 Corinthians 12:3-4, he explains that he was shown paradise: *"And I know such a man – whether in the body or out of the body I do not know, God knows – how he was caught up into Paradise and heard inexpressible words, which it is not lawful for a man to utter."*

The second coming of Jesus Christ

Jesus' second coming was to take some people who believed in Him to soul heaven which is the sixth heaven, also called the psychic realm. Jesus gave a hint of this in John 14:2-3 where he said, *"In My Father's house are many mansions; if it were not so, I would have told you. I go to prepare a place for you. And if I go and prepare a place for you, I will come again and receive you to Myself; that where I am, there you may be also."* The mansions are in soul heaven.

As mentioned earlier, according to Thearc Daniel Arthur, Jesus' second coming was in the year 1956 when He came to establish the soul doctrine. Thearc Daniel Arthur also stated that 1956 was the beginning of the end of the world.

"So Christ was offered once to bear the sins of many. To those who eagerly wait for Him He will appear a second time, apart from sin, for salvation." (Hebrews 9:28)

These include the Christian psychists who sincerely keep both the Father's worship of the Old Testament and the Son's worship of the New Testament where both the body and the spirit are holy.

According to God one must sanctify oneself and be holy for He is holy; keeping our bodies holy is done by keeping the laws of the beasts (Leviticus 11:46). When one is born again, one is given the Holy Spirit which makes the spirit of a person holy. Hence the body is holy and the spirit is also holy. It is this that qualifies a person to go to soul heaven which is the sixth heaven or psychic realm after death.

Matthew 24:27 states: *"For as the lightning comes from the east and flashes to the west, so also will the coming of the Son of Man be."* According to Thearc Daniel Arthur, Christ's first coming was His physical birth in Israel, and His second coming was his spiritual birth in Ghana in 1956. Hence the spirit of Paul, the apostle, was taken to see the heaven paradise being the fourth heaven, which was the limit of Christ's first coming, but the spirit of Thearc Daniel Arthur was taken to see the soul heaven being the sixth heaven which is the limit for Christ's second coming.

Conclusion

The only reason Jesus Christ came to the earth was to save every human being from sin, because sin is the only thing that separates man from God. Because of Adamic sin Adam was separated from God as is confirmed in Isaiah 59:2 *"But your iniquities have separated you from your God, And your sins have hidden his face from you, So that he will not hear."* Since Satan is the source of sin, Jesus had to conquer Satan which He did by His resurrection after death. Therefore, whoever accepts Christ conquers Satan and sin, and whoever continues in sin does not have Christ living in him and therefore is not born again.

CHAPTER 15

WHO IS THE HOLY SPIRIT?

The Holy Spirit is the Spirit of God the Father and the Spirit of Jesus Christ, the Son. He is God in the Trinity. The Holy Spirit is also called the Holy Ghost, the spirit of truth or the comforter as Jesus is recorded as saying in John 14:16-17 & 26: *"And I will pray the Father, and He will give you another Helper, that He may abide with you forever – the Spirit of truth, whom the world cannot receive, because it neither sees Him nor knows Him; but you know Him, for He dwells with you and will be in you… But the Helper, the Holy Spirit, whom the Father will send in My name, He will teach you all things, and bring to your remembrance all things that I said to you."*

The Holy Spirit is the only requirement for anybody to become a Christian. It is obtained only when a person is born again, meaning born of God and the birth is the granting of God's spirit, which is the Holy Spirit.

The dwelling place of the Holy Spirit

The Holy Spirit lives in a person who is born again. Ezekiel 36:27 states: *"I will put My Spirit within you and cause you to walk in my statutes, and you will keep My judgments and do them."* When someone is born again it is confirmed by the Holy Spirit that God puts in the person and is affirmed when that person keeps God's commandments.

In John 14:17 we read: *"The Spirit of truth, whom the world cannot receive, because it neither sees Him nor knows Him; but you know Him, for He dwells with you and will be in you."* True Christians know that the Spirit of God dwells in them and this is why they do not sin deliberately.

Romans 8:9 states: *"But you are not in the flesh but in the Spirit, if indeed the Spirit of God dwells in you. Now if anyone does not have the Spirit of Christ, he is not His."*

Ephesians 2:22 reminds us: *"In whom you also are being built together for a dwelling place of God in the Spirit."* This is further confirmation that the Holy Spirit indeed dwells in one who belongs to Christ and who is a true Christian.

I Corinthians 3:16 asks: *"Do you not know that you are the temple of God and that the Spirit of God dwells in you?"*

How to obtain the Holy Spirit by baptism

In Matthew 3:11 we read that Jesus Christ was baptised with water which led to His spiritual baptism.

Luke 11:13 tells us the Holy Spirit is a gift from God. *"If you then, being evil, know how to give good gifts to your children, how much more will your heavenly Father give the Holy Spirit to those who ask Him!"*

Acts 2:1-4 says, *"When the Day of Pentecost had fully come, they were all with one accord in one place. And suddenly there came a sound from heaven, as of a rushing mighty wind, and it filled the whole house where they were sitting. Then there appeared to them divided tongues, as of fire, and one sat upon each of them. And they were all filled with the Holy Spirit and began to speak with other tongues, as the Spirit gave them utterance."*

In Acts 8:17 we read, *"Then they (Peter and John) laid hands on them, and they received the Holy Spirit."* This is the baptism of the Holy Ghost by impartation.

The Holy Spirit baptism is obtained when an ordained preacher sent by God converts a person and baptises him either in water or by impartation of the Spirit.

The Holy Spirit is received by faith and not by works. In Galatians 3:2 we read: *"This only I want to learn from you: Did you receive the Spirit by the works of the law, or by the hearing of faith?"* It is by the hearing of faith and not by the works of the law that we are made new creatures in Christ.

The power from God

The Holy Spirit brings with Him power, and true Christians are promised they too will receive this power.

"But you shall receive power when the Holy Spirit has come upon you; and you shall be witnesses to Me in Jerusalem, and in all Judea and Samaria, and to the end of the earth." (Acts 1:8)

"Behold, I send the Promise of My Father upon you; but tarry in the city of Jerusalem until you are endued with power from on high." (Luke 24:49)

The spirit imparts gifts to believers. In 1 Corinthians 12:8-10 we're told that these gifts are: wisdom, knowledge, healing, miracles, faith, prophecy, discerning of spirits, tongue speaking and interpretation. The nine gifts of the Holy Spirit demonstrate the power of God as He operates through true Christians.

The Holy Spirit as a teacher

"For the Holy Spirit will teach you in that very hour what you ought to say." (Luke 12:12)

"But the Helper, the Holy Spirit, whom the Father will send in My name, He will teach you all things, and bring to your remembrance all things that I said to you." (John 14:26)

"But when the Helper comes, whom I shall send to you from the Father, the Spirit of truth who proceeds from the Father, He will testify of Me." (John 15:26)

"These things we also speak, not in words which man's wisdom teaches but which the Holy Spirit teaches, comparing spiritual things with spiritual." (1 Corinthians 2:13)

"But the anointing which you have received from Him abides in you, and you do not need that anyone teach you; but as the same anointing teaches you concerning all things, and is true, and is not a lie, and just as it has taught you, you will abide in Him." (1 John 2:27)

Sin against the Holy Spirit

Beware because the Holy Spirit can be taken away from Christians. In Psalm 51 David pleaded with God not to take away the Holy Spirit from him. In 1 Samuel 16:14, the Spirit of the Lord departed from Saul, when he disobeyed God. Beloved, to obey is better than sacrifice, as Samuel told Saul. When Adam and Eve sinned the Holy Spirit was taken away from them. Lucifer and some other angels sinned and they lost God's power in them. We do not want to be like that, so be warned...

"Therefore I say to you, every sin and blasphemy will be forgiven men, but the blasphemy against the Spirit will not be forgiven men." (Matthew 12:31)

"Anyone who speaks a word against the Son of Man, it will be forgiven him; but whoever speaks against the Holy Spirit, it will not be forgiven him, either in this age or in the age to come." (Matthew 12:32)

"But he who blasphemes against the Holy Spirit never has forgiveness, but is subject to eternal condemnation." (Mark 3:29)

"Do not quench the Spirit." (Thessalonians 5:19)

Life with the Holy Spirit

"Likewise the Spirit also helps in our weaknesses. For we do not know what we should pray for as we ought, but the Spirit Himself makes intercession for us with groanings which cannot be uttered. Now He who searches the hearts knows what the mind of the Spirit is, because He makes intercession for the saints according to the will of God." (Romans 8:26-27)

"And such were some of you. But you were washed, but you were sanctified, but you were justified in the name of the Lord Jesus and by the Spirit of our God." (1 Corinthians 6:11)

"I say then: Walk in the Spirit, and you shall not fulfil the lust of the flesh." (Galatians 5:16)

"If we live in the Spirit, let us also walk in the Spirit." (Galatians 5:25)

"It is the Spirit who gives life; the flesh profits nothing. The words that I speak to you are spirit, and they are life." (John 6:63)

"But if you are led by the Spirit, you are not under the law." (Galatians 5:18)

"Now the works of the flesh are evident, which are: adultery, fornication, uncleanness, lewdness, idolatry, sorcery, hatred, contentions, jealousies, outbursts of wrath, selfish ambitions, dissensions, heresies, envy, murders, drunkenness, revelries, and the like; of which I tell you beforehand, just as I also told you in time past, that those who practice such things will not inherit the kingdom of God." (Galatians 5:19-21)

"But the fruit of the Spirit is love, joy, peace, longsuffering, kindness, goodness, faithfulness, gentleness, self-control. Against such there is no law. And those who are Christ's have crucified the flesh with its passions and desires." (Galatians 5:22-24)

Conclusion

The Holy Spirit represents both God the Father and Jesus Christ the only begotten Son of God. It is only the Holy Spirit in man that confirms that man is born again and is a child of God. It is the Holy Spirit in one that makes one holy. The sword of the Holy Spirit is the word of God and therefore He is the genuine interpreter of the Holy Bible, so it is only those who possess the Holy Spirit who give correct interpretation of the Bible. It is only a person who has the Holy Spirit in him who can claim to be a Christian which is affirmed by the sinless life that the person lives.

CHAPTER 16

WHO IS SATAN?

Satan is the great oppressor of people and adversary of God. Satan is the personal name of the devil. "Devil" means slanderer or false accuser. Satan is also identified as the tempter, the wicked one, the ruler of the world, the god of this age and the prince of the power of the air.

Satan is discussed in Ezekiel 28:17 which says, *"Your heart was lifted up because of your beauty; you corrupted your wisdom for the sake of your splendour; I cast you to the ground, I laid you before kings, that they might gaze at you."*

Isaiah 14:13-14 also speaks of Satan: *"For you have said in your heart: 'I will ascend into heaven, I will exalt my throne above the stars of God; I will also sit on the mount of the congregation; On the farthest sides of the north; I will ascend above the heights of the clouds, I will be like the Most High.'"*

These two passages tell of an exalted angelic being (Lucifer), one of God's creatures who became proud, jealous and ambitious. He determined to take over the throne of God for himself, but God removed him from his position of great dignity and honour. Lucifer (Satan) persuaded one third of the angels to join him in his rebellion against God.

Satan was separated from God through sin and therefore God became his enemy. Since then Satan's main objective has been to separate man from God through man's sins. Hence every sin committed by people is caused by Satan so that people would be separated from God in order to follow Satan.

Satan has two kinds of power. He has his own power by virtue of how God created him as an angel with great power and beauty, and he also has power over man and earth — originally given to Adam by God but which Adam lost when Satan caused him to sin.

The work of Satan

Satan's main objective is to separate people from God through their sin (caused by Satan) so that they worship him by their sin instead of avoiding sin to worship God. Any deed of Satan's is therefore directed towards this objective.

Satan aims (i) to prevent people from becoming Christians through sin and worldliness, so that they do not obtain the Holy Spirit and become God's children, and (ii) to persuade Christians who have the Holy Spirit in them to sin in thought, word or deed, in order to lose the Holy Spirit.

Some deeds and characteristics of Satan

Satan blinds the mind of unbelievers. 2 Corinthians 4:3-4 states: *"But even if our gospel is veiled, it is veiled to those who are perishing, whose minds the god of this age has blinded, who do not believe, lest the light of the gospel of the glory of Christ, who is the image of God, should shine on them."*

Satan is the wicked one, as stated in 1 John 5:18-19; *"We know that whoever is born of God does not sin; but he who has been born of God keeps himself, and the wicked one does not touch him. We know that we are of God, and the whole world lies under the sway of the wicked one."*

Satan is permitted to afflict God's people, but he is limited by God and never permitted to win an ultimate victory over Christians as confirmed by the following passages:

- *"And the Lord said to Satan, 'Behold, all that he has is in your power; only do not lay a hand on his person.' So Satan went out from the presence of the Lord."* (Job 1:12)

- *"Many are the afflictions of the righteous, but the Lord delivers him out of them all."* (Psalm 34:19)

- *"These things I have spoken to you, that in Me you may have peace. In the world you will have tribulation; but be of good cheer, I have overcome the world."* (John 16:33)

Satan was to deceive people and tempt them to sin. In Genesis 3:1-6 we see how he lied to Eve by saying God had told them not to eat any fruit of every tree of the garden, whereas God had told them only to refrain from eating the fruit of the tree of the knowledge of good and evil. Satan also deceived them by saying that they would not die, but be as gods. Hence they were tempted to eat the fruit which led to their disobedience to God and therefore to their sin.

Satan also lied, deceived and tempted Jesus three times, but Jesus defeated Satan by using the word of God which is the sword of the Spirit. Satan claims authority over the world, as we see in Luke 4:4-7. When Satan took Jesus to a high mountain and showed Him the kingdom of the world, Satan claimed, *"All this authority I will give You, and their glory; for this has been delivered to me, and I give it to whomever I wish. Therefore, if You will worship before me, all will be Yours."*

Sinners are under the dominion of Satan. Jesus came *"to open their eyes, in order to turn them from darkness to light, and from the power of Satan to God, that they may receive forgiveness of sins and an inheritance among those who are sanctified by faith in Me."* (Acts 26:18)

Satan hinders the gospel. In 1 Thessalonians 2:18 Paul said *"Therefore we wanted to come to you — even I, Paul, time and again — but Satan hindered us."*

Satan steals the word of God from men lest they should believe. Matthew 13:19 tells us, *"When anyone hears the word of the kingdom, and does not understand it, then the wicked one comes and snatches away what was sown in his heart. This is he who received seed by the wayside."*

Satan works counterfeit miracles. In 2 Thessalonians 2:9-10 we read, *"The coming of the lawless one is according to the working of Satan, with all power, signs, and lying wonders, and with all unrighteous deception among those who perish, because they did not receive the love of the truth, that they might be saved."*

Satan sets snares for men to fall into sin. In 2 Timothy 2:26 we're told, *"and that they may come to their senses and escape the snare of the devil, having been taken captive by him to do his will."*

Satan contends with saints. Ephesians 6:12 tells us, *"For we do not wrestle against flesh and blood, but against principalities, against powers, against the rulers of the darkness of this age, against spiritual hosts of wickedness in the heavenly places."*

Satan may inflict disease. Job 2:6-7 reads, *"And the Lord said to Satan, 'Behold, he is in your hand, but spare his life.' So Satan went out from the presence of the Lord, and struck Job with painful boils from the sole of his foot to the crown of his head."*

Satan is a liar and murderer. In John 8:44 we read, *"You are of your father the devil, and the desires of your father you want to do. He was a murderer from the beginning, and does not stand in the truth, because there is no truth in him. When he speaks a lie, he speaks from his own resources, for he is a liar and the father of it."*

Satan opposes the righteous

Paul states in 2 Corinthians 12:7: *"And lest I should be exalted above measure by the abundance of the revelations, a thorn in the flesh was given to me, a messenger of Satan to buffet me, lest I be exalted above measure."*

Zachariah 3:1 says, *"Then he showed me Joshua the high priest standing before the Angel of the Lord, and Satan standing at his right hand to oppose him."*

What can Satan do to a person? Satan can possess a person permanently and use that person in any evil deed unless he's cast out by the power of God. Satan can also possess a person temporarily and use the person to do something evil and then leave the person. Satan cannot possess a Christian because of the Holy Spirit living in him, making his body the temple of God with no room for Satan – unless the Christian is lured to sin. However, Satan has access to any person, be he a Christian or not, in thought, word or deed in the form of temptation such as foolish thoughts, filthy utterances and disreputable deeds.

Satan is the devil and therefore does only evil deeds, as do witches and wizards. Satanism and witchcraft have a common goal of opposing God and God's teachings. The archangel Lucifer and the angels who followed him became Satan and a horde of demons, with Beelzebub being the chief demon. As Satan transformed into a serpent, so too can demons, witches and wizards transform into any form such as birds or even insects and commit their evil deeds.

Methods used by Satan

- Satan often makes people think they are missing out on the good things in life if they do not get involved in all kinds of sin. He tries to disguise sin and sinful pleasures as innocent enjoyment, stirring unholy passions in men and women, causing them to throw away all restraint and live a life of fun, partying and entertainment.

- He keeps the fallen from turning to God and ensures they stay fallen.

- He convinces people to commit suicide; deceiving them by saying it is the best way to end their problems.

- He encourages the "lukewarm Christians" to remain in that situation and eventually backslide further.

- He challenges men to do many things which they would not do under ordinary circumstances, and the men are foolish enough to believe they are not brave if they do not accept his challenges which inevitably lead to trouble.

- He tries to make people think that there is no joy in serving the Lord.

- He urges churches and their leaders to make religion a paying proposition by appealing to the rich and influential through lowering the standard of holy living, making salvation easy for all.

- He encourages people to spend time looking for money and worldly things before they look for God.

Conclusion

Satan is the source of sin. Knowing that sin is the only thing that separates man from God, Satan's strategy is to lure man to sin and thus serve him. The attributes of Satan are completely opposite to the attributes of God because Satan is the opposite of God. Hence Satan's attributes are ungodliness, unrighteousness, unholiness, foolishness, wickedness and the like. Any person who sins therefore serves Satan, but a true Christian is one who serves only God and is therefore sinless.

CHAPTER 17

WHO IS A SAINT?

A saint is one who is holy; one who is separated from worldliness by God for holy use. The word "saint" can be seen as follows:

The *"sa"* stands for sanctified

The *"in"* stands for in

The *"t"* stands for Theo which means God.

So "saint" means "sanctified in Theo" which means "made holy in God". One who is made holy in God is one who has the Holy Spirit living in him because it is only the Holy Spirit which makes one holy. It is only the ones who are born again that have the Holy Spirit living in them, and it is only a true Christian who is born again and therefore has the Holy Spirit and therefore is holy.

Hence every true Christian is basically a saint on earth and continues to be a saint in heaven after death.

Romans 10:15 asks, *"And how shall they preach unless they are sent by God?"*

God only sends the saints to do His work. Hence the preachers, apostles, prophets, evangelists, pastors and teachers must be saints because they are sent by God to do the work and therefore must be sinless.

Whoever is in the clergy and is not sinless has not been sent by God, and therefore does not qualify to be in the clergy. Unfortunately many fall into this category; hence many church goers are not saved because most of the clergy are not truly sent by God.

Ephesians 4:11-12 tells us, *"And He Himself gave some to be apostles, some prophets, some evangelists, and some pastors and teachers, for the equipping of the saints for the work of ministry, for the edifying of the body of Christ."*

Two types of saints

As there are two different heavens which saints can go to after death – paradise and soul heaven – so are there two types of saints. In Luke 23:43 we read that, while hanging on the cross, Jesus told the criminal alongside him, *"Today you will be with Me in Paradise."* In 2 Corinthians 12:4 it is written that Paul was caught up in paradise (fourth heaven). Then Jesus Christ states in John 14:2-3, *"In My Father's house are many mansions; if it were not so, I would have told you. I go to prepare a place for you. And if I go and prepare a place for you, I will come again and receive you to Myself; that where I am, there you may be also."* This is soul heaven (sixth heaven).

As the first coming of Jesus Christ paved the way for the saints to go to heaven paradise, so did the second coming of Jesus Christ pave the way for some saints to go to soul heaven.

The saints who maintain justice and avoid abominations are second-class saints who go to paradise, while the saints who uphold justice and avoid both abominations and ostracism are the first-class saints who go to soul heaven.

Abominations are fornication/adultery, alcohol and smoking which are serious sins that separate people from God to a point that the Holy Spirit will not enter their body. Ostracisms are unclean things eliminated in the soul's version of the holy scriptures. They are the keeping of the laws of the beast for the holiness of the body as written in Leviticus 11.

While on earth the second-class saints have moonlight on them depicting heaven paradise since the light in paradise is the moon, while the first-class saints have sunlight on them depicting soul heaven since the light in soul heaven is the sun. During the first resurrection the second-class saints in heaven paradise will go to soul heaven to join the first-class saints who would be there already and spend eternity together.

Passages confirming who saints are

"Paul, an apostle of Jesus Christ by the will of God, To the saints who are in Ephesus, and faithful in Christ Jesus." (Ephesians 1:1) This message is to all the members of the church in Ephesus, but only the members who are faithful in Christ Jesus are the saints.

"To the church of God which is at Corinth, to those who are sanctified in Christ Jesus, called to be saints." (1 Corinthians 1:2) This affirms that only those members of the church who are sanctified in Jesus Christ are the saints.

"To the saints and faithful brethren in Christ who are in Colosse." (Colossians 1:2) The brethren who are faithful in Christ are saints.

"Paul and Timothy, bondservants of Jesus Christ, To all the saints in Christ Jesus who are in Philippi, with the bishops and deacons." (Philippians 1:1) This reiterates that it is the saints who form the clergy as bishops, deacons, etc.

"Here is the patience of the saints; here are those who keep the commandments of God and the faith of Jesus." (Revelation 14:12) This affirms that saints are those who keep the commandments of God and are faithful in Jesus Christ.

"But fornication and all uncleanness or covetousness, let it not even be named among you, as is fitting for saints; neither filthiness, nor foolish talking, nor coarse jesting, which are not fitting, but rather giving of thanks." (Ephesians 5:3-4) Saints must be sinless in their character.

God loves the saints

"Precious in the sight of the Lord is the death of his saints." (Psalm 116:15) Saints, having been faithful to God and having died in the Lord, please God who rewards them with deserving crowns.

"As for the saints who are on the earth, They are the excellent ones, in whom is all my delight." (Psalm 16:3)

"Now He who searches the hearts knows what the mind of the Spirit is, because He makes intercession for the saints according to the will of God." (Romans 8:27)

"To all who are in Rome, beloved of God, called to be saints." (Romans 1:7)

God rewards His saints

"But the saints of the Most High shall receive the kingdom, and possess the kingdom forever, even forever and ever." (Daniel 7:18)

"Do you not know that the saints will judge the world? And if the world will be judged by you, are you unworthy to judge the smallest matters?" (1 Corinthians 6:2)

"Do you not know that we shall judge angels? How much more, things that pertain to this life?" (1 Corinthians 6:3)

"The mystery which has been hidden from ages and from generations, but now has been revealed to His saints." (Colossians 1:26)

Conclusion

A saint is one who is holy, and holiness only comes from God. Since a true Christian is one who is born again by God and then receives His Holy Spirit, any true Christian possesses the Holy Spirit which makes him holy. Every true Christian is therefore a saint on this earth and will continue to be a saint in heaven after death. However there are two heavens available for saints, heaven paradise (fourth heaven) and soul heaven or the psychic realm (sixth heaven). The saints who avoid ostracism by avoiding pollution of the body (including the law of the beast) are the first-class saints who go to soul heaven. The rest are the second-class saints who go to heaven paradise until the first resurrection when they go to soul heaven for eternal rest.

CHAPTER 18

ONCE SAVED NOT ALWAYS SAVED

When a Christian is saved at one point in time that does not necessarily continue forever.

We must first understand the word "saved" before it can be used appropriately. To save something is to rescue it from harm, danger or loss, to prevent from dying. It is to set someone free from the consequences of sin, to redeem.

Anybody born into the world carries the sinful nature of Adam and Eve. Sin goes back to the fall of Adam and Eve and enslaves all of us and brings death as its wages. Hence Psalm 51:5 states, *"Behold, I was brought forth in iniquity, and in sin my mother conceived me."* For this reason whoever is born into the world must first be saved from the enslavement of sin.

Jesus Christ rightly said that in order to be saved one must be born again. In John 3:3 we're told, *"Most assuredly, I say to you, unless one is born again, he cannot see the kingdom of God."* Jesus Christ further explained in John 3:5 what he meant by "born again": *"Most assuredly, I say to you, unless one is born of water and the Spirit, he cannot enter the kingdom of God."* Here Jesus acknowledges the first birth as being physical and tainted with Adamic sin and the second birth being spiritual and born of God without sin. The confirmation of the second birth is the granting of the Holy Spirit to the individual by God.

A saved person is one who has the Holy Spirit of God, but having the Holy Spirit once does not mean that one always has the Holy Spirit; in fact one can lose it.

The question is, can one who has the Holy Spirit lose it and never have it again? If the answer to that question is yes, then just because you're once saved does not mean you are always saved.

In Psalm 51:11 David begs: *"Do not cast me away from your presence, and do not take Your Holy Spirit from me."* This affirms that the Holy Spirit can be taken away from a person. The Holy Spirit is taken away through sin. For as long as the person continues in sin the Holy Spirit will not be restored and the person would die in sin and go to hell.

In Psalm 51:12 David says, *"Restore to me the joy of Your salvation, and uphold me by Your generous Spirit."* This confirms that when the Holy Spirit is taken away from a person it can also be restored.

Examples of once saved not always saved

1. When Adam was moulded from the dust of the earth by God, and God breathed the breath of life into him and he became a living soul, it was the Holy Spirit granted to him by God that made him a living soul. When Adam sinned the Holy Spirit was taken away from him, hence he became powerless and prone to death.

2. When David sinned through committing adultery the Holy Spirit was taken away from him, but through his repentance it was restored. Unfortunately not all those who received the Holy Spirit but lost it through sin repent and ask for the restoration of the Holy Spirit.

3. Judas Iscariot was a saved apostle of Jesus Christ but by using his love of money against him, Satan enticed him to sin and betray Jesus for thirty pieces of silver. Thus, he was once saved but not always saved because he lost the kingdom of God through sin.

4. It is written in Hebrews 6:4-6: *"For it is impossible for those who were once enlightened, and have tasted the heavenly gift, and have become partakers of the Holy Spirit, and have tasted the good word of God and the powers of the age to come, if they fall away, to renew them again to repentance, since they crucify again for themselves the Son of God, and put Him to an open shame."* This affirms that once saved not always saved.

5. In Hebrews 10:26-29 it is stated: *"For if we sin wilfully after we have received the knowledge of the truth, there no longer remains a sacrifice for sins, but a certain fearful expectation of judgment, and fiery indignation which will devour the adversaries. Anyone who has rejected Moses' law dies without mercy on the testimony of two or three witnesses. Of how much worse punishment, do you suppose, will he be thought worthy who has trampled the Son of God underfoot, counted the blood of the covenant by*

which he was sanctified a common thing, and insulted the Spirit of grace?" This also confirms the idea that just because someone is once saved does not mean they're always saved.

6. Second Peter 2:20-21 says, *"For if, after they have escaped the pollutions of the world through the knowledge of the Lord and Saviour Jesus Christ, they are again entangled in them and overcome, the latter end is worse for them than the beginning. For it had been better for them not to have known the way of righteousness than, after they have known it, to turn from the holy commandments delivered unto them."* This is a serious warning to truly born again Christians that if they go back into sin worse things would happen to them than before they became born again Christians, meaning they would no longer be Christians. This too affirms the policy of once saved not always saved.

7. Ezekiel 18:24 warns the saved Christians as follows: *"But when a righteous man turns away from his righteousness and commits iniquity, and does according to all the abominations that the wicked man does, shall he live? All the righteousness which he has done shall not be remembered; because of the unfaithfulness of which he is guilty and the sin which he has committed, because of them he shall die."* The righteous is a person who is saved, but if he deviates from that path to commit sin and remains in sin until death, he will die unsaved. This means once saved not always saved. Ezekiel 33:13 repeats that premise: *"When I say to the righteous that he shall surely live, but he trusts in his own righteousness and commits iniquity, none of his righteous works shall be remembered; but because of the iniquity that he has committed, he shall die."*

8. In Hebrews 3:13-14 Christians are urged *"exhort one another daily, while it is called 'Today,' lest any of you be hardened through the deceitfulness of sin. For we have become partakers of Christ if we hold the beginning of our confidence steadfast to the end."* Here the saved are being warned to hold fast to their sonship as partakers of Christ lest they are deceived, sin and become unsaved.

9. In Revelation 3:5 Jesus promised that *"He who overcomes shall be clothed in white garments, and I will not blot out his name from the Book of Life; but I will confess his name before My Father and before His angels."* The one who overcomes is one who, after being saved, will continue in righteousness to the end. Whoever breaks the relationship with Christ through sin will have his name removed from the Book of Life. This also backs the premise of once saved not always saved. Jesus promises the saved in Revelation 2:10 *"Be faithful until death, and I will give you*

the crown of life." Being saved is important, but being saved even at the end of one's life is most important because it is only then that one is rewarded with the crown of life. No matter how long one is saved, if it is not up to death the person dies unsaved, hence once saved not always saved.

10. In Mathew 24:12-13 we are forewarned by Jesus about what will happen towards the end of the world. *"And because lawlessness will abound, the love of many will grow cold. But he who endures to the end shall be saved."* We are warned by Jesus Christ that when we're getting to the end of the world sin will be so rampant that many saved Christians will become unsaved, and only those few who remain faithful to the end shall be saved. This confirms that just because we're once saved does not mean we're always saved.

Conclusion

Many are called by God to be His children, but only a few of those called ones are again chosen to be His real children and are therefore saved by God. Consequently, those who are saved are few indeed. Out of the few saved some are deceived by Satan and convinced to sin and lose the Holy Spirit, never regaining it before their death. This happens because Satan's work is twofold: First to prevent people from receiving the Holy Ghost and being saved, and second to deceive the few saved so that they sin and lose the Holy Spirit, and do not get it back again. Hence, once saved not always saved.

CHAPTER 19

LUST

Lust is having a very strong desire to possess something; craving or having a strong passion for something; coveting. It is often associated with wrong strong desires. In a sexual context it is referred to as strong, intense and unrestrained sexual desire or craving for sexual appetite or lasciviousness. It is temptation that leads to lust which brings about sin that ends in death, as it is written in James 1:14-15 *"But each one is tempted when he is drawn away by his own desires and enticed. Then, when desire has conceived, it gives birth to sin; and sin, when it is full-grown, brings forth death."*

Temptation is not sin, but lust is a spiritual sin and the action that follows lust is a physical sin. A physical sin may therefore be a double sin because it may include lust which is a spiritual sin. Lust is the most common sin and sparks the sins of fornication, adultery, envy and hatred.

Everybody is tempted, but a Christian must not be enticed and give in to lust. In 1 Corinthians 10:16 we're told, *"To the intent that we should not lust after evil things as they also lusted."* Any evil thing that one continues to do is done out of lust, hence lust is the most common sin. It is a pre-meditated sin and therefore very serious.

Homosexuality as a form of lust is spoken about in Romans 1:27 – *"Likewise also the men, leaving the natural use of the woman, burned in their lust for one another, men with men committing what is shameful, and receiving in themselves the penalty of their error which was due."* In 1 Corinthians 6:9-10 homosexuality is also mentioned as one of the lusts which will take people to hell: *"Do you not know that the unrighteous will not inherit the kingdom of God? Do not be deceived. Neither fornicators, nor idolaters, nor adulterers, nor homosexuals, nor sodomites, nor thieves, nor covetous, nor drunkards, nor revilers, nor extortioners will inherit the kingdom of God."*

The tenth commandment (Exodus 20:17) condemns lust as follows: *"You shall not covet your neighbour's house; you shall not covet your neighbour's wife, nor his male servant, nor his female servant, nor his ox, nor his donkey, nor anything that is your neighbour's."* This warns that nobody should lust after anything that is not theirs.

Lust of the senses

Our senses have some potential to cause us to lust — the lust of the eye, the ear, the mouth and touch.

Lust of the eye

The lust of the eye is when we desire to possess what we see or to have those who have visual sexual appeal. The first time we lay eyes on a person or an object we'll decide whether it is worth looking at again or not. A Christian abstains from looking at the item again if it appears to be evil or will tempt him to do something evil. Repeatedly looking at what is evil leads to lust and to sin. Pornography is a major lust of the eye; it is evil, destructive and addictive. It was through the lust of the eye that sin first came into the world, as it is written in Genesis 3:6 *"So when the woman saw that the tree was good for food, that it was pleasant to the eyes, and a tree desirable to make one wise, she took of its fruit and ate. She also gave to her husband with her, and he ate."*

Both Adam and Eve sinned because they disobeyed God through the lust of the eye — craving to eat something God had instructed them not to eat. They were tempted when they saw pleasant-looking food, they lusted to eat it and they did eat it which was a sin.

Jesus' third temptation as stated in Matthew 4:8-11 speaks of lust of the eye: *"Again, the devil took Him up on an exceedingly high mountain, and showed Him all the kingdoms of the world and their glory. And he said to Him, 'All these things I will give You if You will fall down and worship me.' Then Jesus said to him, 'Away with you, Satan! For it is written: You shall worship the Lord your God, and Him only you shall serve.' Then the devil left Him, and behold, angels came and ministered to Him."*

When Jesus Christ was tempted through the eye by being shown the kingdoms of the world and the glory of them, Jesus did not lust after them but rather rebuked Satan to get away from Him. Then He quoted the word of God, giving the reason why He would not serve Satan. Then the devil left Him and angels came and ministered to Him.

Lessons to Christians

1. A Christian must expect temptation.
2. Most temptations are the lust of the eye.
3. A Christian must be well equipped with the word of God to be able to apply it at the appropriate time to overcome Satan.
4. A Christian must of necessity act on the word of God to obey God.
5. A Christian who has obeyed God has overcome Satan.
6. Satan is bound to leave the Christian who has resisted him.
7. Angels come and minister to the Christian for the victory.

In Matthew 5:28, Jesus said, *"But I say to you that whoever looks at a woman to lust for her has already committed adultery with her in his heart."* Looking on a woman is not a sin, but it's a potential temptation which a Christian must acknowledge, being careful not to be led into lust which is a sin. This is spiritual fornication which most people commit, including many who claim to be Christians.

There are two types of fornication/adultery. Physical fornication/adultery is where there is physical contact between two people and spiritual fornication/adultery is where there is lust but no physical contact. A true Christian is one who is not guilty of either. Whosoever is guilty of any one of them cannot claim to be a Christian. Lust is the most common temptation, but a true Christian dismisses it immediately and will not be led into sin, whereas a nominal Christian embraces it and enters into sin.

Second Peter 2:14 states: *"having eyes full of adultery and that cannot cease from sin, enticing unstable souls. They have a heart trained in covetous practices, and are accursed children."* Some people live in sin because of what their eyes see and lust after, while others use their eyes to entice others to lust after them. It is only the stable souls of the true Christians which will not be deceived.

In Matthew 20:15 Jesus asks the question: *"Is your eye evil because I am good?"* Anything evil comes from the devil. The evil eye wishes people evil; it bears a grudge and it is full of envy. In 1 John 2:16 we read, *"For all that is in the world — the lust of the flesh, the lust of the eyes, and the pride of life — is not of the Father but is of the world."* This emphasises that all worldliness is evil and that Christians are in the world but must not be of the world. Since God who is in us is greater than Satan who is in the world, we must overcome the world with its evil deeds. (1 John 4:4).

Jesus said in Matthew 6:23, *"But if your eye is bad, your whole body will be full of darkness. If therefore the light that is in you is darkness, how great is that darkness!"* Darkness depicts evil, Satan and hell. Whoever has an evil eye is soaked in sin and therefore completely covered by darkness. Whoever does not have the Holy Spirit is covered by darkness and whoever has the Holy Spirit is covered by either the moonlight or the sunlight, being the light in the fourth heaven (paradise) or the light in the sixth heaven.

In Isaiah 3:16, the Lord said, *"the daughters of Zion are haughty, and walk with outstretched necks and wanton eyes."* Wanton eyes are wicked, immoral and lustful eyes which lead people into sin. Proverbs 6:25 warns: *"Do not lust after her beauty in your heart, nor let her allure you with her eyelids."* This is a genuine and serious warning to Christians since spiritual fornication is one of the most common sins.

David's lust that led to multiple sins is recorded in 2 Samuel 11:2. *"Then it happened one evening that David arose from his bed and walked on the roof of the king's house. And from the roof he saw a woman bathing, and the woman was very beautiful to behold."* This deep lust caused David to commit adultery with Bathsheba and later murder her husband, Uriah. David genuinely repented of his sins and wrote the most effective Psalm for forgiveness – Psalm 51.

The lust of the ear

Just as people look and lust after what they see, so too do people listen and lust after what they hear. There are only two categories of music – godly and worldly. In Ephesians 5:19 we're told we ought to speak to one another *"in psalms and hymns and spiritual songs, singing and making melody in your heart to the Lord"*. A Christian is supposed to sing and listen only to psalms, hymns and spiritual songs, as they attract the angels of God. In contrast, singing or listening to worldly music attracts evil spirits. The lust of the ear includes delighting in hearing gossip and vulgar conversation. Listening to gossip and embracing it often is lust of the ear and must be avoided.

The lust of the mouth

Gossiping and taking delight in flattering and backbiting people are examples of lust of the mouth.

Those who want to be saved are given some guidance in the following passages:

"Lord, who may abide in Your tabernacle? Who may dwell in Your holy hill? He who walks uprightly, And works righteousness, And speaks the truth in his heart; He who does not backbite with his tongue, Nor does evil to his neighbour, Nor does he take up a reproach against his friend." (Psalm 15:1-3)

"Lying lips are an abomination to the Lord." (Proverbs 12:22)

"Deliver my soul, O Lord, from lying lips and from a deceitful tongue." (Psalm 120:2)

In Acts 5:3 Peter said, *"Ananias, why has Satan filled your heart to lie to the Holy Spirit and keep back part of the price of the land for yourself?"* Lying lips and deceitful tongue also refer to the lust of the mouth, with Satan being behind any form of evil.

In Job 15:5-6 it is written: *"For your iniquity teaches your mouth, And you choose the tongue of the crafty. Your own mouth condemns you, and not I; Yes, your own lips testify against you."* It is from the heart that we speak, and lust is from the heart, so what we speak confirms what is in our hearts.

In Luke 19:22 Jesus is quoted as saying: *"Out of your own mouth I will judge you."* This is because what comes out of the mouth exposes what is in the heart. If the mouth utters evil things then the heart, which is the source, is also evil.

To ensure perfect holiness and righteousness in this fourth and last Christian era, a Christian must also avoid eating any food that pollutes the body. (See Leviticus 11.)

The lust of the touch

The lust of the touch includes hand shaking, hugging, kissing and sitting-touching between people of opposite sexes. The longer the touch, the more likely it is to lead on to lust. The lust may emanate from either of the two people or both. To be on the safe side, a true Christian avoids such touches, and if it is sudden and unavoidable it should be brief.

Conclusion

Satan mainly uses the lust of the senses — the eye, ear, mouth and, touch — to lead us into temptation. Temptation is not a sin but it may lead to sin if it is nurtured. Usually the immediate sin is lust which is a spiritual sin, but that may further lead on to physical sin through action. Lust is an uncontrollable desire for something, either good or bad but usually bad and sexual. A true Christian looks up to God in times of temptation, disregards the temptation and is never drawn into lust because of the fear of God. He is strengthened and supported by the Spirit of God in him.

CHAPTER 20

ALCOHOL, SMOKING AND DANCING

This topic is very controversial because diverse views are expressed by real Christians who have the Holy Spirit living in them, nominal Christians who do not have the Holy Spirit and non-Christians. Any true Christian who is filled with the Holy Ghost should always give the benefit of the doubt to God. Where a Christian is uncertain about some habits, a brother or a pastor higher up or more mature in God must be consulted. If they're still in doubt the Christian must pray and fast, appealing to God for guidance and a solution. If, after all that, a Christian is still not sure, they must abstain from the activity.

Alcohol

God created us with a small percentage of alcohol and a large percentage of water in the body. There are two types of drinks in the world – a soft drink and a strong drink. A soft drink is the drink which can never get one drunk no matter the quantity taken. A strong drink is the drink which can get one drunk because of the high alcohol content and the quantity required to get one drunk is unknown, varying from one person to another.

It is a sin for a true Christian with the Holy Spirit in him to take a strong drink knowing perfectly well that it could get him drunk. Please ponder over the following passages meditatively and make up your mind...

In 1 Thessalonians 5:22 we're told, *"Abstain from every form of evil."* Alcohol is an appearance of evil. The evil that alcohol can cause is immeasurable and well known to everybody and that is why a true Christian should abstain from it.

In Matthew 6:13 we read, *"And do not lead us into temptation, but deliver us from the evil one."* A Christian prays about seven times a day mentioning this verse, but in most cases they do not actually meditate on it. Christians do not want to be led into temptation, and yet they often embrace temptation through alcohol. Christians plead with God to be delivered from evil and yet in practice the Christian often compromises their values and ends up doing evil. A Christian must abstain from all appearances of evil, including drinking alcohol.

Romans 14:21 reminds us that *"It is good neither to eat flesh, nor anything whereby thy brother stumbleth, or is offended or is made weak."* A true Christian with the Holy Spirit in him should not allow himself to be enticed to take any alcoholic drink, deceiving himself that he will not get drunk, because a weak brother might follow his example, get drunk and become addicted. The weak in Christ will always quote the strong in Christ who take alcohol.

As we're told in Galatians 5:9, *"A little leaven leavens the whole lump."* Why would a true Christian insist on taking an alcoholic drink knowing full well that it could lead others astray and any good done would be completely tarnished?

When the angel Gabriel announced the conception and birth of John the Baptist to Zachariah (Luke 1:15) he said, *"For he will be great in the sight of the Lord, and shall drink neither wine nor strong drink. He will also be filled with the Holy Spirit, even from his mother's womb."* This affirms that for one to be filled with the Holy Ghost one should not indulge in strong drink, and in the same way one who already has the Holy Spirit must not take strong drink because it may lead to the loss of the Holy Spirit. Simply put, the Holy Spirit and strong drink do not go together. They are incompatible.

Samson's mother was also cautioned by an angel of God not to drink wine or strong drink or eat an unclean thing for the child to be conceived would be a Nazarite unto God from the womb. A Nazarite is a child of God that God uses to perform special duties. A Nazarite is therefore given the Holy Spirit, rendered with power to perform the duty. This confirms that anyone with the Spirit of God should abstain from strong drink.

Supporting passages

Leviticus 10:9 states: *"Do not drink wine or intoxicating drink, you, nor your sons with you, when you go into the tabernacle of meeting, lest you die."* The body of a Christian is the temple of God, and therefore a Christian should not take strong drink.

ALCOHOL, SMOKING AND DANCING

In Isaiah 28:7 we read, *"But they also have erred through wine, and through intoxicating drink are out of the way; The priest and the prophet have erred through intoxicating drink, They are swallowed up by wine, They are out of the way through intoxicating drink; They err in vision, they stumble in judgment."* Taking a strong drink is still condemned because of the problems that it can cause.

Habakkuk 2:15 warns, *"Woe to him who gives drink to his neighbour, Pressing him to your bottle, Even to make him drunk, That you may look on his nakedness!"* If it is sin to give a strong drink to a neighbour, how much more if one takes a strong drink oneself? It is a sin even if a Christian does not take strong drink but keeps strong drink in the fridge for a neighbour.

Proverbs 20:1 states, *"Wine is a mocker, Strong drink is a brawler, And whoever is led astray by it is not wise."* A Christian is being warned here not to be deceived to take strong drink else he will no longer be wise; it is the Holy Spirit in a Christian that makes him wise, for God is the only wise one.

Ephesians 5:18 advises us, *"And do not be drunk with wine, in which is dissipation; but be filled with the Spirit."* This does not mean that one can get drunk but not in excess; the above passages are enough to explain this. If drinking alcohol is forbidden, how much more drunkenness? Alcohol leads to drunkenness and resists the Holy Spirit because one is either filled with the devil or with the Holy Spirit.

Proverbs 31:6 states *"Give strong drink to him who is perishing, and wine to those who are bitter of heart."* A Christian is not perishing but has eternal life, so strong drink is not good for him.

In John 2:1-10 we read of the marriage feast in Cana of Galilee where Jesus turned water into wine. The wine that got finished was strong wine. This was confirmed by the governor of the feast who, after tasting the wine made by Jesus, remarked that it was good and soft wine compared to the original wine; they were different.

In 1 Timothy 5:23 Paul advises Timothy, *"No longer drink only water, but use a little wine for your stomach's sake and your frequent infirmities."* The wine that Paul advised Timothy to take was soft wine because soft wine is medicinal. It has the following medical applications: antiseptic for treating wounds, digestive aid causing diarrhoea and easing pain in child birth. It is also an antioxidant, and lowers the risk for lung, ovarian and prostate cancer. Strong wine, on the other hand, causes cancers including breast, colon and stomach cancer. It also increases the risk for heart disease and cardiac arrhythmias.

If indeed a Christian has the Holy Spirit dwelling in him, he will be convicted by the Holy Spirit that taking a strong drink that can lead to drunkenness is sin. There is no justification for a true Christian to take a strong drink. Any addiction that leads to death is sin. Alcohol leads to death and therefore it is sin to take alcohol.

Smoking

It is sin for a Christian who has the Holy Spirit living in him to smoke. A smoker cannot claim to be a Christian because the Holy Spirit would not occupy such a body. The evil spirit causing such an addiction should first be cast out by impartation of the Holy Spirit before the Holy Spirit can occupy the body. In 1 Corinthians 6:19 readers are asked: *"Do you not know that your body is the temple of the Holy Spirit who is in you, whom you have from God, and you are not your own?"* Since a Christian's body is the temple of God where the Holy Spirit lives, it cannot accommodate smoking.

Romans 12:1 reads, *"I beseech you therefore, brethren, by the mercies of God, that you present your bodies a living sacrifice, holy, acceptable to God, which is your reasonable service."* A Christian has the Holy Spirit and therefore is holy; this holiness should be kept away from smoking and other unholy habits right until the end. Smoking is also an addiction that leads to death. Any evil addiction is uncontrollable because of the evil spirit causing it. A Christian cannot smoke because as it's written in 1 John 4:4 *"…He who is in you is greater than he who is in the world."*

Dancing

Dancing incites lust. It is wrong to lust after another and it is even worse to arouse lust because many people may lust after one who arouses lust, causing them to sin. Dancing may lead to lasciviousness, arousing sexual desires, which lead to one of the most common and serious sins – fornication or adultery.

In 1 Thessalonians 5:22 we are warned thus: *"Abstain from every form of evil."* According to the instruction given in Matthew 6:13, we pray daily: *"And do not lead us into temptation, but deliver us from the evil one."* Dancing can potentially cause us to fail to meet this expectation of a Christian, and it is therefore wrong for any true Christian to indulge in any dancing. Thearc Daniel Kingsley

Arthur who saw God in 1952 gave us some spiritual background to the evil caused through dancing. He said it was through dancing that sin first came into the world, for it was Satan who danced to entice and arouse Eve's sexual desire which led to her having pre-marital sex with Adam. David's dancing was Kabbalistic and so he was permitted to dance. Also remember that David was a Jew and not a Christian. A Christian should not be involved in any worldly dancing.

Conclusion

It is a sin for a true Christian with the Holy Spirit in him to take a strong drink, to smoke or dance. How would a real Christian, uncertain of these bad habits, ignore the warnings and indulge in them rather than giving the benefit of the doubt to what has been written here? A true Christian should avoid them to be absolutely certain to have a place in heaven after death.

CHAPTER 21

HELL

"*Then these will go away into eternal punishment, but the righteous into eternal life.*" (Matthew 25:46) These are the words of the Lord Jesus Christ in one of His teachings on the last judgment.

Eternal punishment takes place in hell (the lake of fire or Gehena), the place of punishment after death for all those who refuse to repent. In the Bible a few different words are used in connection with eternal punishment:

1. Sheol or *"grave"* is used in the Old Testament to mean the place of the dead, generally thought to be under the earth. (See Job 24:19; Psalm 16:10; Isaiah 38:10; Ezekiel 31:17; Amos 9:2.) In sheol the sinful and the righteous are either punished or rewarded.

2. Hades is the Greek word for the underworld, the realm of the dead. It is the word used in the New Testament for sheol. (See Matthew 16:18; Revelation 1:18; 20:13-14.) According to the parable told by Jesus Christ, Hades was a place where good and evil lived close together, but were separated by a chasm. Those who had led a good life on earth were comforted, while those who had not were punished.

3. Gehena, or hell, was named after the valley of Hinnom near Jerusalem where children were sacrificed in a fire to the pagan gods. (See 2 Kings 23:10; 2 Chronicles 28:3.) This is the place of eternal fire (Matthew 5:22; 10:28; Mark 9:49; Luke 12:5; James 3:6; Revelation 19:20) prepared for the devil, his angels and all those who do not believe in God (Revelation 20:9-10). This is the final and eternal state of the wicked after the resurrection and the last judgment.

4. Sheol or Hades was called hell paradise because the righteous were in Abraham's bosom and not suffering and hence in paradise but the sinful were suffering in hell. Those in Abraham's bosom were taken along by Jesus during his resurrection to form heaven paradise.

When Jesus warns against unbelief, He is trying to save us from agonizing, eternal punishment. Hell is a place of everlasting torment after death. It is an everlasting fire prepared for Satan and his angels as well as those who do not obey God absolutely and die in sin. It is eternal damnation and judgment. It is an unquenchable fire. It is a mist of darkness and blackness forever.

This is the summary of what the Holy Bible says about hell. Whoever does not believe in hell does not believe in the word of God and therefore does not believe in God. Hell is real because the Bible says so. If the false Christians, who are indeed called by God but have not availed themselves to be chosen by God because they still continue to commit sin deliberately, knew the unbearable torment and everlasting punishment waiting in hell, they would stop deceiving themselves and surrender completely to lead a sinless life.

God in His infinite mercy occasionally takes the spirits of living people to see hell and return to warn mankind about the torment that awaits in order to scare people off the path that leads to hell. God even responded to the plea made by the rich man in the Bible who asked God to send somebody to the earth to inform people about the reality of hell and heaven, yet people still ignore the warnings and continue to live in sin.

When a person dies there are three spiritual realms where they might go depending on their works on earth. If the person did not die in the Lord, hell paradise (the fourth hell) is their destination of torment until the second resurrection when they will be taken to the seventh hell in the lake of fire for everlasting torment.

Those who die in the Lord will be directed to either heaven paradise which is the fourth heaven in accordance with the first coming of Jesus Christ, or soul heaven which is the psychic realm and sixth heaven where Jesus Christ went to prepare the mansions in accordance with his second coming. During the first resurrection the spirit saints in paradise will be taken to the soul heaven to meet the soul saints and live there for ever.

The reality of hell as a place of punishment or torment

Luke 16:23 states, *"And being in torments in Hades, he lifted up his eyes."* In the following verse the rich man says, *"for I am tormented in this flame"*. The story is about a rich man and Lazarus the beggar confirming the unbearable torment in flames in hell. Subsequently the rich man pleaded with God to send somebody to the earth to warn people about the torment in hell. God has granted that request. People go to hell and come back to warn people on earth, but still even false Christians continue in sin.

Revelation 20:14-15 states, *"Then Death and Hades were cast into the lake of fire. This is the second death. And anyone not found written in the Book of Life was cast into the lake of fire."* The first death takes the unsaved to hell paradise whereas the second death is the second resurrection and final judgment when those in hell paradise, the fourth hell, would be cast into the lake of fire – their final destination for everlasting torment.

In Acts 2:31, after the resurrection, Peter testified about the Christ saying that *"that His soul was not left in Hades"*. This confirms the reality of hell – that Jesus died and went to hell but hell could not prevent Him from being resurrected. During His resurrection Jesus took those in Abraham's bosom (hell paradise) to form heaven paradise.

Hell is real

In Matthew 12:40 we read, *"For as Jonah was three days and three nights in the belly of the great fish, so will the Son of Man be three days and three nights in the heart of the earth."* This tells us the location of hell – that hell is in the earth below us – and it has been scientifically proven that the layer of earth beneath us is molten magma with a very high temperature.

Who goes to hell?

Revelation 21:8 reaffirms that *"the cowardly, unbelieving, abominable, murderers, sexually immoral, sorcerers, idolaters, and all liars shall have their part in the lake which burns with fire and brimstone, which is the second death."* A few unrighteous deeds have been stated here as examples of things that take people to the lake of fire, but it should be seriously noted that any unrighteous deed is sin and takes people to the lake of fire. The "unbelieving" includes false believers who claim to be believers but disobey God. Their final destination is the lake of fire and brimstone which is the second resurrection and second death.

Warning!

Mark 9:43 says this: *"If your hand causes you to sin, cut it off. It is better for you to enter into life maimed, rather than having two hands, to go to hell, into the fire that shall never be quenched."* This is a very serious warning to people to stop anything that would make them sin and lose their place in heaven, ending up in hell where the fire is unquenchable and even the worm does not die. It's very clear that people there will continue to be tormented and be in everlasting pain. If people would only believe in God and therefore believe in his word, nobody on earth would commit sin and go to hell.

Second Peter 2:4 warns us: *"God did not spare the angels who sinned, but cast them down to hell and delivered them into chains of darkness, to be reserved for judgment."* People should know that even if there is one sin in their life at the point of death, that person will be cast down to hell and not be spared.

In John 5:29 we read *"and come forth – those who have done good, to the resurrection of life, and those who have done evil, to the resurrection of condemnation."* This emphasises that true Christians do only that which is good and which qualifies them to go to heaven. False Christians do both good and evil which takes them to hell, along with those who do evil only.

Matthew 7:13-14 states: *"Enter by the narrow gate; for wide is the gate and broad is the way that leads to destruction, and there are many who go in by it. Because narrow is the gate and difficult is the way which leads to life, and there are few who find it."* Indeed very, very, very few people are on the narrow way that leads to heaven. They are the true Christians who have the Spirit of God in them and therefore cannot sin deliberately. And indeed many, many, many people are on the broad way that leads to hell. They are the false Christians and all others who do not have the Spirit of God living in them and therefore cannot stop sinning deliberately. These are the only two ways, there is no middle way. Where do you belong?

Matthew 25:41 tells us, *"Then He will also say to those on the left hand, 'Depart from Me, you cursed, into the everlasting fire prepared for the devil and his angels.'"*

The people on the left are cursed; they are those who continued living in sin, and are therefore sent into everlasting fire.

Conclusion

Hell is real. It is real. It is real! It is an unbearable torment of pain and punishment which is continuous and everlasting. Whoever cannot see the seriousness of hell cannot be a true believer. A true believer of God does not sin deliberately because hell is real to him and he knows one sin in his life will take him to hell. It is very unfortunate that many who claim to be Christians are false and nominal because they are well aware that they commit one or more sins but claim they pray for forgiveness. These people are deceiving themselves because they'll die and go straight to hell – no bend and no curve. It is only people who die in the Lord without sin who escape hell and go to heaven. Be warned, because forewarned is forearmed.

CHAPTER 22

AFFLICTION

Affliction is that which causes or tends to cause bodily pain or mental distress or a spiritual nightmare. Afflictions are unpleasant things which can affect one's body or spirit. They include hardship, torment, sickness, trial, tribulation, misery, persecution, suffering, sorrow, hunger, sickness and punishment.

The source of affliction

Sin is the source of affliction. The first sin which was committed by Adam and Eve brought about affliction. Affliction was the punishment God gave to Adam and Eve when they sinned by disobeying Him, as stated in Genesis 3:16-19.

However it was Satan who caused them to sin. Sin is the major cause of affliction, but Satan is the source of sin. Hence Satan is the major source of affliction.

God allows his children (Christians) to be afflicted, but that affliction is limited to prove his faithfulness to Christians for spiritual upliftment and guidance that will eventually lead the Christians to the heavenly kingdom.

Satan is limited by God in afflicting Christians, but Satan is unlimited when it comes to afflicting nominal Christians and all those who do not believe in God.

Whoever is born into the world is a sinner, so every person falls under affliction.

Passages on afflictions

Affliction caused by sin:

When Adam and Eve sinned God punished them through affliction (Genesis 3:6-16). They did not have affliction in their lives before their sin. Psalm 25:18 says, *"Look on my affliction and my pain, And forgive all my sins."* Psalm 89:32 states: *"Then I will punish their transgression with the rod, And their iniquity with stripes."*

Backsliding may also cause affliction as stated in Psalm 119:67 *"Before I was afflicted I went astray, But now I keep Your word."* In Psalm 119:71 the writer says, *"It is good for me that I have been afflicted, That I may learn Your statutes."*

Examples of impenitence which causes affliction:

- *"And I gave her time to repent of her sexual immorality, and she did not repent."* (Revelation 2:21)

- *"Indeed I will cast her into a sickbed, and those who commit adultery with her into great tribulation, unless they repent of their deeds."* (Revelation 2:22)

- *"Yet man is born to trouble, As the sparks fly upward."* (Job 5:7)

When Adam and Eve were created they did not have any trouble until they sinned. Since then anybody born into this world is a sinner and therefore is born into trouble.

Why is it necessary for Christians to experience afflictions?

Psalm 34:19 states: *"Many are the afflictions of the righteous, But the Lord delivers him out of them all."* Any true Christian is righteous and therefore is bound to have afflictions, but he has the assurance that God will deliver him from all of them.

Acts 14:22 says: *"We must through many tribulations enter the kingdom of God."* Christians are those who qualify to enter into the kingdom of God, so they must go through tribulations.

AFFLICTION

Philippians 1:29 tells us: *"For to you it has been granted on behalf of Christ, not only to believe in Him, but also to suffer for His sake."* Christians are those who believe in Christ and should therefore expect suffering for His sake.

In 2 Timothy 3:12 we read: *"Yes, and all who desire to live godly in Christ Jesus will suffer persecution."* Christians are those who live godly lives in Christ Jesus and therefore must suffer persecution.

Romans 8:17 repeats: *"And if children, then heirs — heirs of God and joint heirs with Christ, if indeed we suffer with Him, that we may also be glorified together."* All Christians are God's children and therefore together with Christ we inherit God — provided we suffer with Christ so that we are glorified with Christ.

In 2 Timothy 2:12 we're told, *"If we endure, We shall also reign with Him. If we deny Him, He also will deny us."* If Christians suffer for Christ's sake they will also reign with Him, but if they deny Him he also will deny them.

In 1 Peter 3:17 we're warned: *"For it is better, if it is the will of God, to suffer for doing good than for doing evil."* It is the will of God that Christians suffer for right doing and not for wrong doing.

James 1:12 reminds us, *"Blessed is the man who endures temptation; for when he has been approved, he will receive the crown of life which the Lord has promised to those who love Him."* Since Christians love the Lord, their blessing is to receive the crown of life if they endured their trials.

Hebrews 12:11 states: *"Now no chastening seems to be joyful for the present, but painful; nevertheless, afterward it yields the peaceable fruit of righteousness to those who have been trained by it."* This means that affliction may lead to righteousness.

We're encouraged in 2 Corinthians 4:17 which tells us that *"Our light affliction, which is but for a moment, is working for us a far more exceeding and eternal weight of glory."*

In 1 Peter 4:14 Christians are told: *"If you are reproached for the name of Christ, blessed are you, for the Spirit of glory and of God rests upon you. On their part He is blasphemed, but on your part He is glorified."*

Promises from God to the afflicted Christians

1. *"Many are the afflictions of the righteous, But the Lord delivers him out of them all."* (Psalm 34:19)
2. *"Blessed are those who are persecuted for righteousness' sake, For theirs is the kingdom of heaven."* (Matthew 5:10)
3. *"My grace is sufficient for you, for My strength is made perfect in weakness."* (2 Corinthians 12:9)
4. *"For in the time of trouble He shall hide me in His pavilion; In the secret place of His tabernacle He shall hide me; He shall set me high upon a rock."* (Psalm 27:5)

Conclusion

Affliction is anything unpleasant causing bodily pain or mental distress or spiritual nightmare or persecution. It was first inflicted on Adam and Eve by God when they sinned against God because they were deceived by Satan. Satan is therefore the source of sin and affliction. A Christian must not be deterred by affliction for it is a necessity that every Christian goes through some affliction which is directed by God.

CHAPTER 23

WHAT IS FORGIVENESS?

Forgiveness is pardon, mercy, reconciliation, peace-making or not bearing a grudge. Forgiveness is an expression of love. It is a person letting go of an offence done against him. It is a genuine spiritual expression of love from the heart of the offended (victim) to the offender. Only God and the person offended know when true forgiveness has indeed taken place. As forgiveness is an expression of love, so unforgiveness is an expression of hatred.

Why should a Christian forgive?

1. Because forgiveness is the basis of Christianity. Since Adam sinned and lost the power of God in him (the soul) there had been a break in the relationship between God and man. Before Christ, man was using the blood of animals to pacify God and ask for forgiveness. This being unsatisfactory, Christ offered to come to the earth to suffer and die so that His blood would pacify God the Father and He would forgive the sin of man. Hence, forgiveness is the foundation of a Christian's deliverance from sin, confirmed by the first utterance of Jesus Christ on the cross: *"Father, forgive them, for they do not know what they do"* (Luke 23:34).

2. Because God has forgiven the Christian.

3. Because the Bible says that a Christian must forgive and a Christian believes in God through the Bible and a Christian must therefore obey this instruction from God.

4. Because a Christian who does not forgive is not yet saved.

5. A Christian who is saved by Christ is one whose sins are forgiven by God through Christ and with the Christian's faith in God; God grants him the Holy Spirit and power to forgive others.

6. The condition laid down by Christ for one to be saved is stated in Matthew 6:12 – *"And forgive us our debts, as we forgive our debtors."*

7. A Christian's prayers (with and without fasting) do not reach God for a response if the Christian has not forgiven all his offenders. This is affirmed by Isaiah 59:2 where we're told: *"But your iniquities have separated you from your God, and your sins have hidden his face from you so that He will not hear."* Psalm 66:18 reiterates this: *"If I regard iniquity in my heart, the Lord will not hear."*

How does a Christian forgive?

Forgiveness is a spiritual exercise from the heart, and the Christian, knowing that it is a condition for his salvation, extends his love for God to the offender and does not bear a grudge. This is a fulfilment of the summary of the laws as stated by Jesus in Matthew 22:37 and 39: *"You shall love the Lord your God with all your heart, with all your soul, and with all your mind"* and *"You shall love your neighbour as yourself."* It's an expression of love towards the offender.

When has a Christian genuinely forgiven the offender?

When the Christian's heart is at peace and his conscience does not condemn him about the unforgiveness; when the offended does not bear any grudge against the offender. If the Christian responds to the offender just as he did before the offence was committed against him, and expresses even more love towards the offender, then he knows he has truly forgiven the one who offended him.

Benefits of forgiveness

There are numerous benefits to forgiving someone, including peace of mind, continued fellowship with the Father, Son and the Holy Ghost, and becoming a child of God. Treasure is laid up in heaven for the Christian, and the possibility of going to hell through unforgiveness is avoided.

When does a Christian forgive?

The Christian must forgive immediately after the offence has been committed, for the longer the Christian delays in forgiving, the more the devil infiltrates the situation and the more the Christian bears a grudge against the offender. This sin breaks the relationship between God and the Christian, so the Christian cannot afford to delay forgiveness.

Some references on forgiveness

Matthew 5:7 states: *"Blessed are the merciful, for they shall obtain mercy."* A Christian who forgives is the one who is merciful and therefore is blessed by God, and God, in turn, will show mercy by forgiving the Christian's sins.

In Matthew 5:9 we read: *"Blessed are the peacemakers for they shall be called the sons of God."* A Christian who forgives is a peacemaker and is blessed by God who makes him His child. Whoever does not forgive is not a child of God.

Matthew 5:23-24 reminds us that, *"If you bring your gift to the altar, and there remember that your brother has something against you, leave your gift there before the altar, and go your way. First be reconciled to your brother, and then come and offer your gift."* It is imperative that a true Christian forgives immediately when he is offended, because a true Christian prays several times a day and for as long as he has not forgiven any offence done against him, none of his prayers offered will reach God. A person who has not reconciled with his brother is a person who has not forgiven his brother.

Matthew 5:44-45 summarises what Jesus says is expected of a true Christian: *"But I say to you, love your enemies, bless those who curse you, do good to those who hate you, and pray for those who spitefully use you and persecute you, that you may be sons of your Father in heaven; for He makes His sun rise on the evil and on the good, and sends rain on the just and on the unjust."*

Love, bless, do good and pray for one another means forgive. Therefore a Christian is to forgive his enemies, forgive those who curse him, forgive those who spitefully use him and persecute him. In other words a Christian must always forgive when offended in order to qualify to become a child of God.

Jesus again emphasises forgiveness in Matthew 6:14-15 when He says, *"For if you forgive men their trespasses, your heavenly Father will also forgive you. But if you do not forgive men their trespasses, neither will your Father forgive your trespasses."* A Christian is one whose sins have been forgiven by God, and who forgives when offended. It is these two that confirm that a person is a Christian. A Christian whose sin is forgiven by God is empowered by the Holy Spirit to easily forgive others when offended.

In Matthew 18:21-22 we're told, *"Then Peter came to Him and said, 'Lord, how often shall my brother sin against me, and I forgive him? Up to seven times?' Jesus said to him, 'I do not say to you, up to seven times, but up to seventy times seven.'"* Seventy times seven (70 x 7) is equal to 490. Jesus' answer is metaphorical; He is simply saying that a true Christian must always forgive.

Jesus emphasised this again in Mark 11:25 when he said, *"And whenever you stand praying, if you have anything against anyone, forgive him, that your Father in heaven may also forgive you your trespasses."* A person who has not forgiven others who have offended him cannot claim to be a Christian because God will not forgive him his sins since he has not forgiven others.

Ephesians 4:32 reiterates that: *"And be kind to one another, tender-hearted, forgiving one another, even as God in Christ forgave you."* This repeats that when one is forgiven by God, through the precious blood of Jesus on the cross, one has to forgive everybody who offended them before one can claim to be a Christian.

In Luke 23:34 Jesus said on the cross: *"Father forgive them; for they do not know what they do."* It was a plea for mankind to be forgiven, confirmed by the shedding of Jesus' blood to glorify God that indeed led to the forgiveness of mankind by God.

Conclusion

Jesus pleaded with God the Father to forgive mankind, and He shed His blood, dying as a prerequisite for God to accept the sacrifice that would ensure forgiveness of mankind's sins. God the Father accepted Christ's sacrifice and forgave us. The Holy Spirit in a Christian empowers the Christian to forgive others. Hence, a genuine Christian is the one whose sins have been forgiven by God through Jesus Christ and who forgives all others who offend him, empowered to do this because of the Holy Spirit living in him.

CHAPTER 24

CHRISTIAN PRAYER

In 1 Thessalonians 5:17 we are enjoined to pray without ceasing. Prayer is a spiritual exercise, it is not just a shopping list of requests we present to God. Prayer involves entering into a relationship with God – establishing a link with God. If we become aware of this it will not be difficult for us to pray more often. If your prayer is always a shopping list, and if you ask for the same things over and over again, you'll soon become tired. If you always strive to think of what to ask for and it doesn't come easily, it becomes difficult to pray. If that's the way you approach prayer, then when there are no immediate needs the urge to pray is not there.

Prayer is a powerful exercise for spiritual development. Since we are made for spiritual growth, we must not stop praying. A Christian communicates to God through prayer through Jesus Christ who is the mediator. God also communicates with Christians through his word through Jesus Christ.

How do we pray?

Our Lord Jesus Christ prayed often and in Matthew 6 He taught us how to pray. He stressed the need to pray in solitude and not to use vain repetitions as the heathen do. Then He offered a model prayer – the Lord's Prayer.

It starts in Matthew 6:9 saying: *"Our Father in heaven, hallowed be Your name."* This emphasises the reality of heaven because it is the dwelling place of God and rekindles the idea of everlasting life which we hope to spend with Him in heaven through our Lord Jesus Christ. It also emphasises the need to give praises to God always. We should start our prayer, therefore, with praises and thanksgiving.

Matthew 6:10: *"Your kingdom come, your will be done. On earth as it is in heaven."* Indeed, the kingdom has come! This is the time – Jesus Christ has come to dwell in us in the form of the Holy Ghost. Now the Father, Son and Holy Ghost live in us, the true Christians.

The kingdom of God is a way of life, and to acquire it requires total surrender to the will of God. To get it something must give, and that is the abandonment of outward things; in short, self-surrender. Give up those things which shackle the spirit, divide its interests and deflect it on its road to God, whether these things be riches, habits, religious observances, friends, interests, distastes or desires. Here it is attitude not actions that matter. In spiritual terms we call this poverty of spirit. Spiritual poverty then is a mental rather than a material state. It is the poor in spirit, not the poor in substance, who are to be spiritually blessed and inherit the kingdom of God.

Matthew 6:11: *"Give us this day our daily bread."* In other words, we're saying, "Give us today the food we need." There are seven days in a week and each day has its food. The seven days represent the seven churches of God as well as the seven spirits of God. (See Revelation 1:4 – *"John to the seven churches which are in Asia, and from the seven spirits who are before his throne."*)

The Spirit of God is the Holy Spirit. The Holy Spirit was sent to the seven churches at different times. The Holy Spirit was first sent to the first church, the Catholic Church. The Holy Ghost was then sent to the second church, the protestant churches, and others followed until the charismatic and spiritual churches and finally the seventh grade of the Holy Spirit was sent to the seventh church, which is the last Christian church, the path of Jesus Christ's second coming where the soul gospel is preached. The food of the seventh day of the week is Psychism, the doctrine of the soul which dwells on both the Old and the New Testaments and emphasises justice, abominations and ostracism.

Matthew 6:12: *"And forgive us our debts (trespasses) as we forgive our debtors."* Whoever is converted or born again has his sins forgiven by God. It is only when one's sins are forgiven that one can receive the Holy Ghost. Any true Christian who possesses the Holy Spirit and does not forgive others when offended loses the Holy Spirit because it is impossible for that one to go to heaven. Going to heaven is conditional on your sins being forgiven by God and you too forgiving others' sins. Hence Jesus Christ warns those whose sins are forgiven not to sin anymore. But because we are human and therefore prone to sin, anytime we go to God in prayer we must ask for forgiveness of not only our presumptuous sins, but also our secret sins. (See Psalm 19:12-13.)

Matthew 6:13a: *"And do not lead us into temptation, but deliver us from the evil one."* This comes immediately after the confession of our sins. So that we do not fall back into sin, we plead for strength to be able to withstand temptation because we are tempted when we are enticed by our own lust. God allows us to be tempted but He assures us that He will not allow us to be tempted beyond our human strength and will make a way for us to overcome the temptation provided we look up to Him. Hence He delivers us from the evil or sin that we might have committed.

Matthew 6:13b: *"For thine is the kingdom, and the power and the glory forever. Amen."* Kingdom means "king's domain"; this is where the king dwells. God is the only king so the kingdom belongs to God. All power belongs to God; all glory belongs to God. Amen means "so be it".

From the Lord's Prayer we may identify the following as the formula for praying:

- Start with praise and thanksgiving.
- Surrender completely to the will of God.
- Confess your sins.
- Make your petition/request.
- Ask for protection as you live your daily life.
- End the prayer with thanksgiving, believing that your request has been granted.

When and how often should we pray?

Pray in the morning as stated in Psalm 5:3 *"My voice You shall hear in the morning, O Lord; In the morning I will direct it to You, and I will look up."*

Pray day and night as it's written in Psalm 88:1 *"O Lord, God of my salvation, I have cried out day and night before You."*

Pray morning, noon and evening as we read in Psalm 55:17 *"Evening and morning and at noon, I will pray, and cry aloud, and He shall hear my voice."*

Pray all night, as we read in Luke 6:12 *"Now it came to pass in those days that He went out to the mountain to pray, and continued all night in prayer to God."*

In 1 Thessalonians 5:17 we're told, *"Pray without ceasing."*

Pray at midnight. *"At midnight I will rise to give thanks to You, because of Your righteous judgments,"* we read in Psalm 119:62.

"Seven times a day I praise You, Because of Your righteous judgments," it says in Psalm 119:164.

In Matthew 26:41 the Lord Jesus Christ enjoins us to *"Watch and pray, lest you enter into temptation."* Again in Mark 13:33 the Lord repeats, *"Take heed, watch and pray; for you do not know when the time is."* The two suggest that we should pray quite often. In fact, in Luke 18:1 the Lord again advises *"that men always ought to pray and not lose heart",* which is also reiterated by Paul in Ephesians 6:18 with his advice that we should be *"praying always with all prayer and supplication in the spirit".*

A true Christian must therefore pray many times in a day. There are also routine prayer periods which are related to circumstances but not time per se, so a true Christian should find time to pray when he/she wakes up in the morning. Every true Christian must observe a quiet time every day, preferably first thing in the morning. This is the time when we thank God for watching over us the previous night when we were asleep and dedicate ourselves to Him for the rest of the day. After talking to God we allow Him to also talk to us by reading His word and meditating on it. Similarly, we should find time to pray in the night before we go to bed. This is when we thank God for taking care of us and our loved ones throughout the day, noting in particular our lapses and asking for forgiveness and bringing ourselves under the umbrella of God's care in the depths of the night.

It is recommended that any Christian who wants to develop spiritually make it a practice to observe mid-night prayers. Although they're called mid-night prayers they can be undertaken any time between 12 midnight and 3am. This is a common practice in the Thearchical Domain Church. In Acts 16:25 it is recorded that in prison Paul and Silas prayed at midnight and a great miracle ensued; any Christian who wants a breakthrough in spiritual upliftment must routinely engage in midnight prayers.

Other circumstances also require that we pray — these may include before leaving home for work; when we get to our work place and before starting work; before we leave our work place; when we get home; and when we are about to eat. In routine prayer we often kneel down and go into some form of meditation, focusing the mind on things in silence, but in most of the circumstantial prayers we do what is known as *"ejaculatory"* or instant prayer. An example is found in Genesis 24:12-14 where the servant sent to go and look for a wife for Isaac prayed on the spur of the moment and God answered his prayer. It must be noted that the servant was working within certain preordained conditions and so God's hands were readily at work. Similarly, if we want our prayers to be heard we must fulfil certain conditions.

Conditions for answered prayers

Everyone who prays to God hopes that their prayer will reach God and that God will answer the prayer. Below I list some of the conditions set by God through His word which need to be fulfilled in order for prayers to reach Him and to be answered.

Believe and have faith in God

Matthew 21:22 says, *"And whatever things you ask in prayer, believing, you will receive."* Belief is a precondition for one's prayers to receive a positive answer from God, bearing in mind that the believer is one who obeys God. Hence it is the prayer of the born again Christian which is answered by God. In Hebrews 11:6 Paul adds, *"But without faith it is impossible to please Him, for he who comes to God must believe that He is, and that He is a rewarder of those who diligently seek Him."*

In James 1:6 it is written, *"But let him ask in faith, with no doubting, for he who doubts is like a wave of the sea driven and tossed by the wind."* Faith in God is also a prerequisite for a prayer to reach God and get a positive response. We are saved by grace through faith, so it is only those who are saved who do have faith in God. And those who are saved cannot deliberately sin.

Do not commit sin

Mark 11:25 states, *"And whenever you stand praying, if you have anything against anyone, forgive him, that your Father in heaven may also forgive you your trespasses."* Refusing to forgive someone is a common sin which is an obstacle for our prayers to reach God and receive an answer.

John 9:31 reminds us that *"Now we know that God does not hear sinners; but if anyone is a worshipper of God and does His will, He hears him."* God hears only the prayers of a true Christian who does not sin deliberately; God does not hear the prayers of a sinner. If there is one sin in someone's life that the person is aware of, that one sin alone prevents God from hearing the prayer because the person still disobeys God.

1 Peter 3:12 reiterates, *"For the eyes of the Lord are on the righteous, and His ears are open to their prayers; But the face of the Lord is against those who do evil."* The righteous are the true Christians who cannot sin and therefore their prayers are heard by God, while the evil doers are the false Christians who commit sin and therefore their prayers are not heard by God.

Proverbs 15:29 reaffirms that, *"The Lord is far from the wicked, but He hears the prayer of the righteous."* This emphasises that righteousness – the sinlessness of a Christian – is the key to one's prayers being heard by God.

Psalm 66:18 states *"If I regard iniquity in my heart, the Lord will not hear."* Any person who prays to God but knows that he is committing a sin, that person is being told here and now that God does not hear the prayer that he offers to Him.

Proverbs 28:9 says that *"One who turns away his ear from hearing the law, even his prayer is an abomination."* This means whoever does not obey the law of God, his prayer is sin or hateful to God because disobedience of the law is disobedience to God. We are reminded in 1 John 3:4 that *"Whoever commits sin also commits lawlessness, and sin is lawlessness."* It is very important that a true Christian becomes conversant with the laws of God, because it is only by knowing them that we can keep them. If we don't know them we will always be going against them and that will be imputed to us as sin, thereby impeding our prayers.

In Isaiah 59:2 it is stated *"But your iniquities have separated you from your God; And your sins have hidden His face from you, so that He will not hear."* It is the sin of Adam that separated man from God. Christ died to take away this sin from those who believe in Him. Whoever commits sin, even if it is only one, is separated from God and God will not hear him. Just one sin in a person's life before death blocks them from entering into the kingdom of God.

The following verses reassure us that the prayers of true Christians are heard and answered by God.

- *"If you abide in Me, and My words abide in you, you will ask what you desire, and it shall be done for you."* (John 15:7)

- *"And whatever we ask we receive from Him, because we keep His commandments and do those things that are pleasing in His sight."* (1 John 3:22)

- *"Now this is the confidence that we have in Him, that if we ask anything according to His will, He hears us."* (1 John 5:14)

- *"And whatever you ask in My name, that I will do, that the Father may be glorified in the Son."* (John 14:13)

Receive the Holy Spirit

In John 4:23 we read, *"But the hour is coming, and now is, when the true worshippers will worship the Father in spirit and truth; for the Father is seeking such to worship Him."* It is only when the Holy Spirit is given to a person that they can worship in Spirit and in truth and that their prayers are heard by God.

John 4:24 repeats that, *"God is Spirit, and those who worship Him must worship in spirit and truth."* This reaffirms that it's essential for a Christian to obtain the Holy Spirit to enable him to worship in spirit and for his prayers to be heard by God.

Pray without doubt

James 1:5-8 cautions: *"If any of you lacks wisdom, let him ask of God, who gives to all liberally and without reproach, and it will be given to him. But let him ask in faith, with no doubting, for he who doubts is like a wave of the sea driven and tossed by the wind. For let not that man suppose that he will receive anything from the Lord; he is a double-minded man, unstable in all his ways."*

In Matthew 21:21-22 Jesus said, *"Assuredly, I say to you, if you have faith and do not doubt, you will not only do what was done to the fig tree, but also if you say to this mountain, 'Be removed and be cast into the sea,' it will be done. And whatever things you ask in prayer, believing, you will receive."* A lot thus depends on our frame of mind when we pray. In this case, we must not doubt because *"Faithful is He that calleth you, who also will do it"* (1 Thessalonians 5:24).

All the conditions listed above are necessary for a Christian to be able to reach God through prayer and receive a positive response. Nonetheless, as human beings our best may not be good enough to appear in perfect condition before God.

In Romans 8:26-27 Paul reminds us that God, by His infinite grace, blesses the little effort we make with the intercession of the Holy Spirit: *"Likewise the Spirit also helps in our weaknesses. For we do not know what we should pray for as we ought, but the Spirit Himself makes intercession for us with groanings which cannot be uttered. Now He who searches the hearts knows what the mind of the Spirit is, because He makes intercession for the saints according to the will of God."* What God therefore wants from us is for us to desire to please him and then He will reward our effort with the blessings of the Holy Spirit.

Above all, it is important for Christians to remind themselves that *"There is one God, and one mediator between God and men, the man Christ Jesus; who gave Himself a ransom for all, to be testified in due time"* (1 Timothy 2:5). Hence Jesus Himself said in John 14:13-14: *"And whatever you ask in My name, that I will do, that the Father may be glorified in the Son. If you ask anything in My name, I will do it."* In our prayers we always ask God the Father for something. Jesus is reminding us of the necessity of asking in His name, because He is the mediator, and then we will receive what we ask for.

All that has been said here is true and sincere and may God approve it according to His will.

Conclusion

It is the true believer in God, having the Holy Spirit living in him and who therefore should not sin wilfully, whose prayer is heard and answered by God.

CHAPTER 25

CHRISTIAN FASTING

In narrow terms fasting refers to the discipline of abstaining from food for spiritual reasons (spiritual discipline), but broadly it includes abstaining from all other bodily pleasures, mainly sex. Although it is often linked with prayer, fasting is a spiritual discipline on its own. It is a continuous prayer without words.

Fasting is denying the physical body food for a period of time in order to raise the spiritual level over and above the physical lust. Another purpose is to purge the body of any pollution it might have come into contact with. Fasting serves to clean the body and make room for the Spirit of God to rejoice in the temple within the body.

Forms of fasting

There are three main forms of fasting presented in the Bible:

- The normal fast – abstaining from all solid or liquid food. If this is done for a day the fasting is from 6am to 6pm.

- The absolute (dry) fast – abstaining from both food and water, day and night for a number of days. (See Esther 4:16 and Acts 9:9.) Normally this type of fast should not be done for more than three days, otherwise the kidneys may start to shut down and the body dehydrate. Moses and Elijah undertook the absolute fast for forty days and forty nights, but only under supernatural conditions. (See Exodus 34:28; Deuteronomy 9:9 and Kings 19:8.)

- The partial fast (or moderation) – basically a restriction of diet rather than complete abstention (Daniel 10:3). There are variations on this fast including fruit fasting, liquid fasting and others. It is often recommended for people who are old or have health problems.

Importance of fasting

Fasting is important in the Christian's life because Christ Himself practised it. He fasted for forty days and forty nights (Matthew 4:2). He taught that it should be part of a Christian's devotion and an act of preparation for His return (Matthew 9:15). He warned, however, that we should do it only for the right reasons, not from a selfish desire for praise (Matthew 6:16-17). Fasting strengthens our prayers to God, particularly when they pertain to a very serious problem. Fasting assists prayer in preventing or reducing unforeseeable problems and dangers. It is a catalyst to prayer.

It is advisable that every true Christian who indeed has the Spirit of God in him and wishes for a progressive spiritual upliftment should observe some fasting. A Christian who does not fast cannot reach the optimum spiritual potential required of him. Jesus Christ fasted to enable us to imitate Him. Moses, David, John the Baptist, the prophets and prophetesses and apostles of Jesus Christ all fasted, so how can a true Christian ignore fasting?

In Mark 9:29 Jesus said, *"This kind can come out by nothing but prayer and fasting."* Jesus said this after healing the boy possessed by the deaf and dumb spirit which the apostles could not cast out. It shows the extra power obtained from fasting in order for our prayers to be more effective.

Matthew 4:2 tells us, *"And when He had fasted forty days and forty nights, afterward He was hungry."* Jesus Christ prayed for us to pray and He fasted for us to fast. Whoever prays to God must also fast for spiritual upliftment. Just like with prayer, only those who do the will of God can rest assured that God will see their fasting and reward them. We fast to experience hunger and to derive spiritual benefits as we subject the body to a temporary suffering. Jesus felt the hunger, but people want to fast without being hungry.

After the fasting Satan tempted Jesus and Jesus overcame the trial. The lesson is that fasting reinforces our level of power so that we're able to overcome trials.

In Luke 5:33 the scribes and Pharisees asked Jesus Christ, *"Why do the disciples of John fast often and make prayers, and likewise those of the Pharisees, but Yours eat and drink?"* In Luke 5:35 Jesus replied, *"But the days will come when the bridegroom will be taken away from them; then they will fast in those days."* Those days are now. With this teaching from Jesus about fasting, what other further teaching would Christians need to be convinced that fasting is a necessity and not an option?

Some advice on fasting is given to a Christian couple in I Corinthians 7:5 which reads, *"Do not deprive one another except with consent for a time, that you may give yourselves to fasting and prayer; and come together again so that Satan does not tempt you because of your lack of self-control."* (This refers to an inability to control sexual desire.) This warning to a couple to refrain from sex during fasting shows the involvement of holiness in fasting and the extra power that fasting generates.

Judges 20:26 tells us, *"Then all the children of Israel, that is, all the people, went up and came to the house of God and wept. They sat there before the Lord and fasted that day until evening."* This reiterates the necessity for fasting. In this case it was one day of fasting and the duration was from morning till evening.

In Esther 4:16 Esther said, *"Go, gather all the Jews who are present in Shushan, and fast for me; neither eat nor drink for three days, night or day."* For any very important decision or any serious problem every true Christian must resort to prayer supported by fasting. Esther's fasting was a three-day dry fast without food or water from the morning of the first day till the evening of the third day.

In 2 Corinthians 11:27 where Paul recounts some of his activities, he says, *"In weariness and toil, in sleeplessness often, in hunger and thirst, in fastings often, in cold and nakedness."* This affirms how often a true Christian should fast.

It pays to make fasting a regular practice in the life of the Christian. In the Thearchical Domain Church we fast twice a week, on Wednesdays and Saturdays. We fast on Wednesdays, the middle of the week, to remind ourselves of God and our duty towards Him. We also use it to strengthen ourselves spiritually and to position ourselves so that we will be able to arrest any unforeseen problem. When he's dealing with a foreseeable problem or need the Christian may decide to fast for three, seven, fourteen, twenty-one, forty or even more days according to the gravity of the problem. This too we do in the Church individually and often as a group.

The Saturday fasting is mainly to prepare us spiritually for Sunday service when we go to meet God. The essence is such that we shall be worthy recipients of the blessings God has prepared for His children on the special day.

The purposes of fasting with prayer

There are ten main purposes for fasting with prayer:

1. To honour God. (Zechariah 7:5; Luke 2:37)
2. To humble ourselves before God. (Ezra 8:21; Psalm 69:10; Isaiah 58:3)
3. To mourn over personal sin and failure. (1 Samuel 7:6; Nehemiah 9:1-2)
4. To mourn over the sins of the church, nation and world. (1 Samuel 7:6; Nehemiah 9:1-2)
5. To seek grace for a new task and to reaffirm our consecration to God. (Matthew 4:2)
6. To seek God by drawing near to Him and persisting in prayer against opposing spiritual forces. (Judges 20:26; Ezra 8:21,23,31; Joel 2:12)
7. To show repentance and so make a way for God to change His declared intentions and judgment. (2 Samuel 12:16, 22; 1 Kings 21:27-29; Joel 2:12-14; Jonah 3:5,10)
8. To save people from bondage to evil. (Isaiah 58:6; Matthew 17:14-21)
9. To gain revelation and wisdom concerning God's will. (Isaiah 58:5-6,11; Daniel 9:3,21-22; Acts 13:2-3)
10. To open the way for the outpouring of the Spirit and Christ's return to earth for His people. (Matthew 9:15)

Conclusion

It is rather unfortunate that some Christians obey God and want their prayers and fasting requests to reach Him but, since they take fasting lightly, they lose the spiritual benefits that come from it. Jesus said *"This kind can come out by nothing but prayer and fasting"* (Mark 9:29). This shows there is a limitation to prayer in some encounters and fasting is a catalyst to solve some of those problems. Hence, to obtain the optimum spiritual benefit a true Christian must live a fasted life by fasting regularly. On the other hand there are some false Christians who regularly pray and fast seriously but their prayers and fasting do not reach God because they continue to live in sin.

CHAPTER 26

CHRISTIAN MARRIAGE

Before marriage

It is essential for a true Christian to pray and fast regularly for the specific purpose of asking God for the appropriate marriage partner. Every Friday I used to fast and pray for a wife and God showed me my wife clearly in a dream one night.

A true Christian should never make the mistake of marrying someone they are not sure is also a true Christian. In 2 Corinthians 6:14 we're told: *"Do not be unequally yoked together with unbelievers. For what fellowship has righteousness with lawlessness? And what communion has light with darkness?"* Should a Christian desire to marry an unbeliever, the Christian must make sure that the unbeliever is genuinely converted and has become a true believer before they commit to the marriage, otherwise the Christian does that at his/her own peril.

Your marriage partner will either support you to enable you to serve God better and be drawn closer to God, or will ruin you and draw you away from God. The most important thing for us to achieve on earth is to be born again and to become a child of God. Ecclesiastes 12:13 affirms this: *"Fear God and keep His commandments; for this is man's all."* The next important thing is to get a marriage partner who will support you in fearing God and help you to keep God's commandments.

The three major reasons for a Christian to marry are:

1. To avoid fornication (1 Corinthians 7: 2)
2. To have a help meet (Genesis 2:18)
3. To reproduce (Genesis 1:28)

In I Corinthians 7:2 it is stated: *"But since sexual immorality is occurring, each man should have sexual relations with his own wife, and each woman with her own husband."* This affirms that a true Christian should not fornicate and therefore no true Christian should engage in pre-marital sex. This is because fornication is among the most serious sins, for most sins that a person commits are outside the body, but fornication is within the body. Sex is meant for only the married – husband and wife.

God regards any sexual act between any two people of opposite sex as marriage, no matter the age. In John 4:17-18 we read the story of Jesus meeting a woman at Jacob's well and asking her to call her husband. *"'I have no husband,' she replied. Jesus said to her, 'You are right when you say you have no husband. The fact is, you have had five husbands, and the man you now have is not your husband. What you have just said is quite true.'"* Here Jesus meant that the woman had had sexual relations with five different men already and the sixth one with whom she was having a sexual relationship at the time was still not her husband but only a boyfriend.

Hebrews 13:4 tells us *"Marriage should be honoured by all, and the marriage bed kept pure, for God will judge the adulterer and all the sexually immoral."* A Christian should never fornicate before marriage. It is very serious and may affect them getting the perfect marriage partner.

Proverbs 18:22 reads: *"He who finds a wife finds what is good and receives favour from the Lord."* God approves of marriage and it is a blessing for a Christian to marry after consulting God for guidance.

Genesis 2:18 tells us: *"It is not good for the man to be alone. I will make a helper suitable for him."* This means that marriage was instituted by God so that the partners would support each other and, above all, go to heaven. Just as in her creation Eve was shown to be a part of Adam through being formed from Adam's rib, so in marriage man and woman are brought together to be one, in oneness and in service to God. It is only God who knows a Christian's marriage partner and who can ensure they are paired up to marry the perfect partner.

All the requirements of marriage and a formal approval of the marriage by parents or church must be fulfilled before the couple-to-be can come together.

The ideal and most convenient marriage is where both Christians belong to the same church, having the same Lord, doctrine, faith and baptism. If possible the two must agree on one church where both can worship after marriage, because no two church denominations are the same. There are differences among all churches.

There are often people who are against specific marriages for various reasons. For example someone else may have wished to marry the bride or groom. It is thus very important for the Christians to be fully armed in the Lord through prayer and fasting.

The couple-to-be should bear in mind that Christians marry for good and may not break their marriage in accordance with the word of God in Matthew 19:6 which says, *"Therefore what God has joined together, let no one separate."* Please do not enter into marriage until you are absolutely certain you have the right partner.

After marriage

Ephesians 5:21-28 clearly summarises what is expected of a husband and wife.

"Submitting to one another in the fear of God." The wife submits to the husband and husband also submits to the wife in their obedience to God.

"For the husband is head of the wife, as also Christ is head of the church; and He is the Saviour of the body." The wife should acknowledge that the husband is the head of the family and must consult the husband where necessary and whenever she's in doubt. The husband must realise that he represents Christ in the family.

"Therefore, just as the church is subject to Christ, so let the wives be to their own husbands in everything." The wife should rely or depend on the husband as the church depends on Christ.

"Husbands, love your wives, just as Christ also loved the church and gave Himself for her." The husband must love the wife to the extent that he must be prepared to die for her, because Christ loved the church so much so that he died for the church.

The husband, representing Christ and being the leader has greater responsibility than the wife. This means the husband must apply God's law in guiding the wife. Should the husband go against God's law, the wife has the right to respectfully remind him of what the Bible says. There must be a mutual respect and love between the husband and wife. The husband earns his respect and acceptance of leadership from the wife by obeying God, and the wife earns her love from the husband by her obedience to him through God's law.

"For this cause shall a man leave his father and mother, and shall be joined unto his wife, and they two shall be one flesh" (Ephesians 5:31). It is God's desire that man and woman marry and become one, so in marriage man and woman are brought together again to be one, just as Adam and Eve were separated in creation when the rib that formed her was taken from his side, but married to become one again.

Mark 10:9 tells us, *"What God has joined together let not man put asunder."* Christian marriage is therefore permanent and the union should not be broken. It may only break according to God's guidance where there is adultery or obstacles in the marriage preventing one from serving God in the best way possible.

In a Christian marriage God is the third person; no other person should be allowed to interfere in the marriage. The Christian couple should always look to God for the solution of every problem. Should it be necessary for consultation from a pastor, a friend or relative about an issue in the marriage, that should be the last resort.

There must be mutual trust between husband and wife. There must be a transparency in everything they do and there must not be anything that one would wish to hide from the other. A Christian couple prays together and individually. The couple avoids apportioning blame for any mistake either of them makes. Do not scold your spouse but rather sympathise and empathise for any mistake done. A Christian spouse must admit any wrong done and sincerely apologise, and the apology must be sincerely accepted by the other spouse.

A Christian couple should never ever insult each other or make any insinuating remarks or gestures, like frowning. The couple must avoid arguing and quarrelling. Under no circumstance should the husband hit his wife and vice versa.

Anger is one of the major tools that Satan uses to bring discontentment between husband and wife. Anger is bound to be present at various times, but prolonged anger leads to sin. In Ephesians 4:26 we're told, *"Be angry and do not sin."* *"Swift to hear, slow to speak, and slow to wrath,"* is the advice found in James 1:19. When one is angry one should not speak lest unpleasant remarks are made which aggravate the situation.

Satan uses anger to break a Christian's communication with God, and that break lasts for as long as the anger persists. Anger is one of the measuring factors to show the level of a Christian's closeness to God; the closer one is to God the shorter the duration of anger. A Christian must use his level of anger to determine his spiritual level and development with God.

Unforgiveness is another sin often seen in marriages that Satan uses to break a Christian's relationship with God. As long as unforgiveness is harboured in a Christian their communication with God is non-existent. The Christian couple must forgive each other instantly when one is offended. The period for unforgiveness should never be long because as long as there is unforgiveness prayers offered to God do not reach Him. Unforgiveness is another scale used for measuring a Christian's spiritual growth and maturity; the quicker a Christian forgives when offended, the higher their spiritual level in God.

Psalm 66:18 states: *"If I regard iniquity in my heart the Lord will not hear."* The Christian couple must be faithful to God and to each other; never hiding anything within their hearts otherwise their prayers will never reach God.

There must be freedom of expression in the relationship since both partners are adults. They should be able to take decisions individually and collectively; under no circumstances should there be suppression or oppression of one towards the other.

Serious warnings to Christian couples are found in I Corinthians 7:3-5: *"Let the husband render to his wife the affection due her, and likewise also the wife to her husband. The wife does not have authority over her own body, but the husband does. And likewise the husband does not have authority over his own body, but the wife does. Therefore, do not deprive one another except with consent for a time, that you may give yourselves to fasting and prayer; and come together again so that Satan does not tempt you because of your lack of self-control."*

The above passage means the following: The couple should not deny each other in their sexual relationship unless there is a very tangible reason. It is imperative that the husband and wife pray and fast from time to time, and the couple should refrain from sex whenever they are fasting. The couple should come together again after the period of fasting lest Satan uses that period of separation to tempt either of them to sin, perhaps because of their inability to control their sexual desire. The spiritual importance of a person's holiness in a time of fasting is affirmed here.

Why man is the head of woman

From the creation Adam was created before Eve and therefore he's older and deserves to be the head.

Woman means woven from man or taken out of man (Genesis 2:23) or part of man. Only Adam's rib was taken to create Eve and the rest of the body belonged to Adam, and therefore Adam deserved to be the head.

Eve was created from the rib, being the middle portion of Adam's body and not from the crown of his head or the sole of his feet. Woman is therefore neither the head nor the tail of man, but rather his partner and help meet (Genesis 2:18).

The following passages reaffirm the headship of husband in marriage:

- When Adam and Eve sinned God said to Eve, *"I will greatly multiply thy sorrow and conception, in sorrow thou shalt bring forth children, and thy desire shalt be to thy husband, and he shall rule over thee."* (Genesis 3:16)

- First Corinthians 11:3 states, *"But I want you to know that the head of every man is Christ, the head of woman is man, and the head of Christ is God."*

- Ephesians 5:23 reads, *"For the husband is head of the wife, as also Christ is head of the church; and He is the Saviour of the body."*

In practice

Man proposes marriage to woman; this shows that man is the leader of the marriage and consequently the leader of the woman.

It is the man who pays the bride's price or dowry for the marriage, showing leadership.

In normal marriages it is noted that men are usually older in age than women and therefore deserve to be leaders.

Following on from these reasons there is no doubt that the husband is the leader and partner of the wife, but not her oppressor.

Conclusion

The couple's first allegiance is to God and the next is to each other. The Christian couple must trust God wholly and acknowledge Him first in everything they do. There must be mutual trust between them. The couple should always look to God for solutions and not allow anybody else to infiltrate their marriage. They should not disclose their marriage secrets to anybody. They must carefully weigh any advice on marriage given by relatives, friends or pastors and eventually take their own decision, fully depending on God.

CHAPTER 27

THE SOUL

Soul originated in the creation of man Adam as we're told in Genesis 2:7, *"And the Lord God formed man of the dust of the ground, and breathed into his nostrils the breath of life; and man became a living soul."* Soul is therefore life. God is life and Jesus is life and the breath of life is the Holy Spirit that God gave Adam so that he would be like the Father (God), the Son (Jesus Christ) and the Holy Spirit (the comforter).

Jesus Christ said in John 14:6, *"I am the way, the truth, and the life. No one comes to the Father except through Me."* If Jesus Christ is the life and soul is life then it is Jesus Christ who gave life to the soul. Whoever has the soul has life and therefore has Jesus Christ living in him. Whoever does not have Christ living in him therefore does not have real soul and, though physically alive, is spiritually dead. Soul is the life of the spirit; without the soul, the spirit is lifeless.

When Adam was formed of the dust of the ground, he was motionless and it was the breath of life that brought life into him, making him a soul with life. Soul is therefore a combination of material (physical, dust) and immaterial (spiritual, the Holy Spirit). Body and spirit are not mentioned in the creation, but they are within the soul. The soul is the combination of the supernatural spirit, which is the Holy Spirit in man, the natural spirit which is the ordinary spirit in man and the material body of man.

When Adam and Eve sinned they lost the supernatural spirit which was the Holy Spirit in them and therefore lost power – the life in them – and found themselves to be naked, stripped of the power of God in them.

Soul is immortal and mortal, immaterial and material or undying and dying. It is the spark of God, the power of God, the Spirit of God in man which is the real soul. Man became a living soul because of the Spirit of God in man. However in the world the word *"soul"* is widely used for any person with or without God's spirit in them.

Psalm 51:1 reads, *"Behold, I was shapen in iniquity; and in sin did my mother conceive me."* Because of Adamic sin which led to the withdrawal of the Holy Spirit, everybody who is conceived is born without the Holy Spirit which is the soul; hence whoever is born into the world does not possess the real soul. The two exceptions to this are Jesus Christ who was conceived by the Holy Spirit and John the Baptist who received the Holy Spirit while in his mother's womb.

Psalm 23:3 states: *"He restores my soul; He leads me in the paths of righteousness For His name's sake."* This reaffirms that everybody born into the world is without a soul. It is only a person who is born again and therefore has the Holy Spirit living in him whose soul has been genuinely restored. Very few people in the world have had their souls truly restored. When the soul is restored then a Christian is led on the path of righteousness by God to live a sinless life to please God.

In Ezekiel 18:4 and 18:20 we read, *"The soul who sins shall die."* This refers to the mortal soul that dies because the immortal soul does not die. The mortal soul sins but the immortal soul does not sin. The Spirit with God is immortal soul and has life, and the spirit without God is mortal soul and lifeless.

Angels are only spirits, but human beings are both spirit and body. Angels are immaterial and immortal, just as human beings with God in them are material and immortal, but humans without God in them are material and mortal.

Hebrews 4:12 states: *"For the word of God is living and powerful, and sharper than any two-edged sword, piercing even to the division of soul and spirit, and of joints and marrow, and is a discerner of the thoughts and intents of the heart."* Soul is spirit, but a special spirit which matches the Spirit of God. It is only the word of God which allows us to tell the difference between soul and spirit.

Christians are warned in 1 Peter 2:11 as follows: *"Beloved, I beg you as sojourners and pilgrims, abstain from fleshly lusts which war against the soul."* Fleshly lust is sin and the soul in a Christian is the Spirit of God which abhors sin; therefore, when a Christian indulges in fleshly lust he commits sin and cannot stay connected with the soul.

Matthew 16:26 reminds us of the importance of the soul: *"For what profit is it to a man if he gains the whole world, and loses his own soul? Or what will a man give in exchange for his soul?"* Soul is the most important thing because it is the soul that gives life to man, and without it man is lifeless. Nothing can be compared to it; it is life. God has set before man life and death – the only two choices – and whichever man genuinely desires is given to him. If man chooses Christ, he has chosen life and God grants him the soul. If man chooses worldliness he has chosen death and therefore does not have the real soul.

According to Thearc Daniel Kingsley Arthur, *"The soul is the celestial body in man which Adam lost in the Garden of Eden, upon which derivation brought in the Education, the embankment of all holy vibrations, Adytum or the most sacred part of the temple or body that we bear. The frame of man is composed of three elements: the body, spirit and soul. The soul is the standard of man, the purpose of which education consists of four divisions: physical, intellectual, moral and spiritual in search of the great lost treasure of man, but never at all can mind replace the soul as the mind is only an entrance to the soul. The doctrine of the soul is psychism. Piety and sanctity are the perpetuity of the soul. Within the soul is the excellence of wisdom and intellectuality."*

Conclusion

Soul is life. It is the breath of life, which is the Spirit of God, which God breathed into Adam that made him a living soul. Out of this came the spirit and body. When Adam sinned, that life which is the real soul was taken away and therefore Adam and Eve remained with only the spirit and the body, and without the soul. Consequently anybody born into this world arrives without the soul and therefore does not have spiritual life because God does not live in him. They are living physically, but are spiritually dead. When one is born again the soul is restored. Whoever is born into the world has an empty soul and a lifeless spirit. Whoever is born again has real soul and a spirit with life because it is the soul that gives life to the spirit. Whoever has the soul cannot sin deliberately.

CHAPTER 28

WHY A TRUE CHRISTIAN SHOULD NOT WORRY

A true Christian is a Christian who is genuinely born again and therefore has the Holy Spirit living in him; he should not sin deliberately because he obeys God.

Proverbs 3:6 reminds us: *"In all your ways acknowledge Him, And He shall direct your paths."* A true Christian consults God on every decision he takes and therefore does not worry since God directs his path to achieve what is best for him.

In 1 Thessalonians 5:18 we're commanded: *"In everything give thanks; for this is the will of God in Christ Jesus for you."* Since God is concerned about his children, as you are, in whatever situation you find yourself whether pleasant or unpleasant, give thanks to Him and do not worry for He will provide you with what is appropriate for you.

Psalms 46:10 says, *"Be still, and know that I am God."* God gives assurance to Christians not to worry for He is the Almighty God in control of every situation.

In 1 John 3:22 we're reassured: *"And whatever we ask we receive from Him, because we keep His commandments and do those things that are pleasing in His sight."* A true Christian indeed keeps the commandments of God and pleases God by his obedience to God, and therefore whatever he asks from God, he receives. If the Christian does not receive it, he should not worry because if for some reason God does not approve of the request, it may be harmful to the Christian.

In 1 John 4:6 we're told, *"We are of God. He who knows God hears us; he who is not of God does not hear us. By this we know the spirit of truth and the spirit of error."* Since Christians are God's children, those who are also Christians understand them. If those who are not God's children do not understand us we should not worry.

In Matthew 6:25-32 Jesus assures true Christians not to worry about their lives, or what they will eat, drink or wear, for even the fowls of the air who do not do any work are fed by Him and are also clothed even more beautifully than King Solomon.

Matthew 6:33 reminds us: *"But seek first the kingdom of God and His righteousness, and all these things shall be added to you."* True Christians are those who have sought the kingdom of God and His righteousness, and Jesus assures us that all things shall be given to us. Why then should Christians worry?

Ecclesiastes 12:13 tells us, *"Let us hear the conclusion of the whole matter: Fear God and keep His commandments, For this is man's all."* A true Christian fears God and keeps his commandments and therefore fulfils his purpose for coming into the world. Why then should a true Christian worry?

Philippians 4:6 encourages us thus: *"Be anxious for nothing, but in everything by prayer and supplication, with thanksgiving, let your requests be made known to God."* This is the assurance from God that a true Christian should not worry about anything as long as he makes his requests known to God.

Matthew 7:21 tells us, *"Not everyone who says to Me, 'Lord, Lord,' shall enter the kingdom of heaven, but he who does the will of My Father in heaven."* A true Christian does the will of God and therefore qualifies to go to heaven, so why should he worry?

In 1 John 3:9 we see that *"Whoever has been born of God does not sin, for His seed remains in him; and he cannot sin, because he has been born of God."* A true Christian cannot sin deliberately and therefore is born of God. Why should you worry if you are God's child?

In John 3:3 Jesus tells the man, *"Most assuredly, I say to you, unless one is born again, he cannot see the kingdom of God."* A true Christian is born again and therefore can go to heaven so he has no need to worry.

This is repeated in John 3:5 when Jesus says, *"Most assuredly, I say to you, unless one is born of water and the Spirit, he cannot enter the kingdom of God."* A true Christian is born of water and spirit and hence qualifies to go to heaven.

In Proverbs 15:29 we're told, *"The Lord is far from the wicked, But He hears the prayer of the righteous."* A true Christian is righteous and therefore God hears his prayer; why worry then?

Romans 8:16 says, *"The Spirit Himself bears witness with our spirit that we are children of God."* A true Christian is sure that the Spirit of God bears witness with his spirit that he is a child of God.

Jesus said in John 16:33, *"These things I have spoken to you, that in Me you may have peace. In the world you will have tribulation; but be of good cheer, I have overcome the world."* Jesus gives us the assurance that it is only in Him that Christians can have peace. He warns Christians that we are bound to have problems in the world, but we should not worry because He is in control of the world.

Psalm 66:18 warns us: *"If I regard iniquity in my heart, The Lord will not hear me."* A true Christian does not regard iniquity in his heart and therefore the Lord hears him. Why then should a Christian worry?

Luke 12:32 assures us, *"Do not fear, little flock, for it is your Father's good pleasure to give you the kingdom."* The kingdom is already given to you as a true Christian, so there's no need to worry.

In Isaiah 41:10 we are soothed as follows: *"Fear not, for I am with you; Be not dismayed, for I am your God. I will strengthen you, Yes, I will help you, I will uphold you with My righteous right hand."* With this assurance from God, a Christian should not worry.

Jesus also gave this assurance to His disciples in Luke 12:22: *"Therefore I say to you, do not worry about your life, what you will eat; nor about the body, what you will put on."* Jesus tells Christians that they will never be in want.

Conclusion

Christians are granted the best on earth and the best in heaven, including eternal life; hence a Christian should never worry.

CHAPTER 29

LOVE

God is love and all love emanates from God; love is the major attribute of God. Love is an intense feeling of affection and genuine belief in Jesus Christ. It includes both unconditional and conditional love from God.

Physical love

Physical, natural love is an intense feeling and affection that's expressed through action. Every normal human being born into the world has feelings of affection and therefore has physical love. This love is inborn because one is born with it; it is therefore unconditional love from God.

Family love

This is the love between parents and their children, or among the members of a family. This familial love which occurs naturally is called storge.

Friendship love

This is the love expressed by people who live truer and fuller lives by relating to each other authentically and teaching each other about the limitations of their beliefs and defects in their character. This friendship love is called philia.

Sexual love

This is the love due to physical attraction and behaviour leading to a desire for sexual intimacy. This sexual love is called eros.

Spiritual love

Spiritual love is a love for a genuine belief in Jesus Christ as stated in John 3:16 *"For God so loved the world that He gave His only begotten Son, that whosoever believes in Him should not perish, but have everlasting life."* Spiritual love is therefore a conditional love from God and only applies to the children of God – Christians whose souls have been restored and therefore have the Holy Spirit living in them. They have the spiritual love which is the agape love – charity or sacrificial love – which is the love of God for man and of man for God.

1. Agape love indicates the nature of the love of God

    - Towards His Son, Jesus Christ.

        "Jesus said, I have declared to them your name and will declare it: that the love wherewith you have loved me may be in them and I in them." (John 17:26)

    - Towards the human race.

        "For God so loved the world, that He gave His only begotten Son, that whosoever believes in Him should not perish, but have everlasting life." (John 3:16)

        "But God commends His love toward us, in that, while we were yet sinners Christ died for us." (Romans 5:8)

    - Toward those who believed on the Lord Jesus.

        "He that has my commandments, and keeps them, he it is that loves me: and he that loves me shall be loved of my Father, and I will love and will manifest myself to Him." (John 4:21)

2. Agape love conveys God's will to His children

    "A new commandment I give to you, that you love one another, as I have loved you that you also love one another. By this shall all men know that you are My disciples if you have love one to another." (John 13:34-35)

3. Agape love also expresses the essential nature of God

    - *"He who does not love does not know God, for God is love."* (1 John 4:8)

    - Love can be recognised by the actions it prompts as seen in God's love in the gift of His Son as stated in 1 John 4:9-10: *"In this was manifested the love of God towards us, because that God sent His only begotten Son into the world that we might live through Him. Herein is love, not that we loved God, but that He loved us, and sent His only Son to be the propitiation for our sins."*

    - Love found its perfect expression in the Lord Jesus. Christian love is the fruit of the Spirit of Jesus in the believer. *"But the fruit of the Spirit is love, joy, peace, long-suffering, gentleness, truth, meekness, temperance; against such there is no law."* (Galations 5:22-23)

    - Love enables us to run our lives according to God's commandments. *"I will run the way to your commandments, when you shall enlarge my heart."* (Psalm 119:32)

    - Without such love we are nothing. *"And though I bestow all my goods to feed the poor, and though I give my body to be burned and have not charity, it profits me nothing."* (1 Corinthians 13:3)

    - Such Spirit-inspired love never fails but always flourishes. *"Charity never fails; but whether there be prophecies, they shall fail; whether there be tongues, they shall cease; whether there be knowledge, it shall vanish away."* (1 Corinthians 13:8)

Brotherly Love

Brotherly love is used to express the love of Christians for one another, since all Christians are sons of the same Father – God.

"Be kindly affectioned one to another with brotherly love in honor, preferring one another." (Romans 12:10)

"Let brotherly love continue." (Hebrews 13:1)

"And to godliness brotherly kindness; and to brotherly kindness charity." (2 Peter 1:7)

"Honor all men. Love the brotherhood. Fear God. Honor the King." (1 Peter 2:17)

"Finally be ye all of one mind, having compassion one for another, love as brethren, be pitiful, be courteous." (1 Peter 3:8)

"For whosoever shall do the will of my Father which is in heaven, the same is My brother and sister and mother." (Matthew 12:50)

A Christian's love should also extend beyond the Christian brotherhood to touch all people. *"For if you love them which love you, what reward have you? Do not even publicans the same? And if you salute your brethren only, what do you more than others? Do not even the publicans so?"* (Matthew 5:46-47)

A Christian should even love his enemies as Jesus said in Matthew 5:44-45, *"Love your enemies, bless them that curse you, do good to them that hate you and pray for them which despitefully use you and persecute you. That you may be the children of your Father which is in heaven: For He makes His sun to rise on the evil and on the good and sends rain on the just and on the unjust."*

Love is supreme

"And now abides faith, hope, charity, these three, but the greatest of these is charity." (1 Corinthians 13:13)

"The grace of the Lord Jesus Christ and the love of God, and the communion of the Holy Ghost be with you all. Amen." (2 Corinthians 13:14) In this great benediction it is the love of God that leads to the grace of Jesus Christ and the communion of the Holy Ghost.

How to love

- With all the heart, soul and mind. *"Jesus said unto the pharisee, you shall love the Lord your God with all your heart, and with all your soul and with all your mind."* (Matthew 22:37)

- As one loves himself. *"You shall love your neighbour as yourself."* (Matthew 22:39)

- Not in word but in deed. *"My little children, let us not love in word, neither in tongue; but in deed and in truth."* (1 John 3:18)

- As Christ loves us. *"This is my commandment. That you love one another as I have loved you."* (John 15:12)

- Without hypocrisy. *"Let love be without dissimulation."* (Romans 12:9)

- With genuine love. *"By pureness, by knowledge, by long-suffering, by kindness, by the Holy Ghost, by love unfeigned."* (2 Corinthians 6:6)

- Sincerely. *"I speak not by commandment, but by occasion of the forwardness of others, and to prove the sincerity of your love."* (2 Corinthians 8:8)

- Enough to lay down one's life for others. *"Greater love has no man than this that a man lay down his life for his friends."* (John 15:13)

- By being of service to one another. *"For, brethren, you have been called to liberty: only use not liberty for an occasion to the flesh, but by love serve one another."* (Galatians 5:13)

- Forbearing (tolerating) one another. *"With all lowliness and meekness, with long-suffering, forbearing one another in love."* (Ephesians 4:2)

- With a pure heart, fervently. *"Seeing you have purified your souls in obeying the truth through the spirit to unfeigned love of the brethren, see that you love one another with a pure heart fervently."* (1 Peter 1:22)

- Without fear. *"There is no fear in love; but perfect love casts out fear: because fear has torment. He that fears is not made perfect in love."* (1 John 4:18)

- More than the love between parents and children. *"He that loves father or mother more than Me is not worthy of Me, and he that loves son or daughter more than Me is not worthy of Me."* (Matthew 10:37)

Conclusion

Love is the supreme attribute of God. God is love and the source of every kind of love. Man's love is twofold and emanates from God. It is a feeling of affection and belief in God. The feeling of affection is inborn — a love granted to every normal human being by God. This love from God is unconditional; it is a physical love that all mankind exhibits. The belief love is not inborn and it is only granted by God to those who believe in God through Jesus Christ. It is therefore conditional and spiritual, and is exhibited only by Christians.

CHAPTER 30

THE BLOOD

Blood is life and soul is life. Blood is the life of the flesh and soul is the life of the spirit. Blood is the life of the flesh or body of man and animals. Blood was needed for our sanctification and to appease God in an attempt to get forgiveness for man's sin, but the blood of animals was not enough to pacify God. God, however, being merciful, sent His only begotten son Jesus Christ to shed His precious blood on the cross for perfect appeasement and sanctification.

The following passages affirm this:

- *"Whom God set forth as a propitiation by His blood, through faith, to demonstrate His righteousness, because in His forbearance God had passed over the sins that were previously committed."* (Romans 3:25)

- *"In the same manner He also took the cup after supper, saying, "This cup is the new covenant in My blood. This do, as often as you drink it, in remembrance of Me."* (1 Corinthians 11:25)

- *"But now in Christ Jesus you who once were far off have been brought near by the blood of Christ."* (Ephesians 2:13)

- *"In whom we have redemption through His blood, the forgiveness of sins."* (Colossians 1:14)

- *"And by Him to reconcile all things to Himself, by Him, whether things on earth or things in heaven, having made peace through the blood of His cross. His blood brings peace between God and man which is reconciliation or restoration of father and son relationship."* (Colossians 1:20)

- *"But into the second part the high priest went alone once a year, not without blood, which he offered for himself and for the people's sins committed in ignorance."* (Hebrews 9:7)

- *"For if the blood of bulls and goats and the ashes of a heifer, sprinkling the unclean, sanctifies for the purifying of the flesh, how much more shall the blood of Christ, who through the eternal Spirit offered Himself without spot to God, cleanse your conscience from dead works to serve the living God?"* (Hebrews 9:13-14) It is the blood that purges our conscience from the worldliness of serving Satan to the godliness of serving God.

- *"Therefore, brethren, having boldness to enter the Holiest by the blood of Jesus, by a new and living way which He consecrated for us, through the veil, that is, His flesh."* (Hebrews 10:19-20) The blood of Jesus cleanses us thoroughly from all unrighteousness, making us sinless and able to enter the holiest area of spiritual development.

- *"To Jesus the Mediator of the new covenant, and to the blood of sprinkling that speaks better things than that of Abel."* (Hebrews 12:24)

- *"And so Jesus also suffered outside the city gate to make the people holy through His own blood."* (Hebrews 13:12) People are made holy through the blood of Jesus.

- *"Now may the God of peace, who through the blood of the eternal covenant brought back from the dead our Lord Jesus, that great Shepherd of the sheep, equip you with everything good for doing His will, and may He work in us what is pleasing to Him, through Jesus Christ, to whom be glory for ever and ever. Amen."* (Hebrews 13:20-21)

- *"But with the precious blood of Christ, a lamb without blemish or defect."* (1 Peter 1:19)

- *"This is the one who came by water and blood – Jesus Christ. He did not come by water only, but by water and blood. And it is the Spirit who testifies, because the Spirit is the truth. For there are three that testify: the Spirit, the water and the blood; and the three are in agreement."* (1 John 5:6-8) Jesus Christ came into the world by physical birth through Mary as well as spiritual birth through the Holy Spirit, but all the people of the world came by physical birth only, hence all people must be born again.

- *"For the life of a creature is in the blood, and I have given it to you to make atonement for yourselves on the altar; it is the blood that makes atonement for one's life."* (Leviticus 17:1) The soul is the life of the spirit and was lost by the sin of Adam, while the blood is the life of the flesh which is used to bring reconciliation and represent the soul.

- *"In fact, the law requires that nearly everything be cleansed with blood, and without the shedding of blood there is no forgiveness."* (Hebrews 9:22) The nature of God requires the shedding of blood for forgiveness, hence before the coming of Jesus Christ the blood of animals was used, but through His death on the cross His blood was shed for the forgiveness of sin. After the shedding of Jesus' blood on the cross, one has to wholly accept Jesus Christ and be born again before one's sins are forgiven. Hence Jesus repeatedly warns the born again not to sin anymore.

- *"In Him we have redemption through His blood, the forgiveness of sins, in accordance with the riches of God's grace."* (Ephesians 1:7) It is the precious blood that Jesus shed on the cross that pacified God and brought about the forgiveness of mankind's sins so that whosoever would genuinely accept Christ would be redeemed through His blood.

- *"But be sure you do not eat the blood, because the blood is the life, and you must not eat the life with the meat."* (Deuteronomy 12:23) The reason why a Christian should not eat the blood of an animal is because the blood is the life of the flesh and therefore immortal, but the flesh is mortal and can be eaten.

- *"Keep watch over yourselves and all the flock of which the Holy Spirit has made you overseers. Be shepherds of the church of God, which he bought with his own blood."* (Acts 20:28) All who have been called and chosen by God to do His work in the church are warned to be very serious as He saved the church by the loss of His life through the blood He shed on Calvary.

- *"Since we have now been justified by His blood, how much more shall we be saved from God's wrath through Him!"* (Romans 5:9)

- *"But if we walk in the light, as He is in the light, we have fellowship with one another, and the blood of Jesus, His Son, purifies us from all sin."* (1 John 1:7)

- *"And from Jesus Christ, who is the faithful witness, the firstborn from the dead, and the ruler of the kings of the earth. To him who loves us and has freed us from our sins by his blood."* (Revelation 1:5)

Functions of Jesus' blood

The summary of the functions of the blood of Jesus is as follows:

1. For the remission of sin. (Matthew 26.28)
2. For the purchasing and feeding of the church. (Acts 20:28)
3. For the justification and saving of the believer. (Romans 5:9)
4. For purging the conscience from dead works to serve the living God. (Hebrews 9:14)
5. For redemption as a lamb without blemish and without spot. (1 Peter 1:19)
6. For cleansing us from all sin. (1 John 1:7)
7. For washing us of our sins. (Revelation 1:5)
8. For washing and making the robes of the believer white. (Revelation 7:14)
9. For enabling the brethren to overcome Satan. (Revelation 12:11)
10. For drawing us closer to God. (Ephesians 2:13)
11. For reconciling mankind to God. (Ephesians 2:13)
12. For sanctification. (Hebrews 13 12)
13. For redemption and forgiveness of sins. (Colossians 1:14)
14. For peace and reconciliation unto Himself. (Colossians 1:20)

In Genesis 4:10 the Lord said, *"What have you done? Listen! Your brother's blood cries out to Me from the ground."* The blood is the soul of a person, representing the person in the spiritual realm.

Conclusion

Blood is the soul of the flesh. It gives life to the flesh; just as the soul gives life to the spirit and without it a person will be living but spiritually dead because the person will not have the Holy Spirit. The blood of Jesus is the soul of Jesus which is the Holy Spirit.

CHAPTER 31

BLESSING

Blessing is favour or grace from God. God is the only source of blessing; any blessing without God is no blessing. The greatest blessing from God is His forgiveness of mankind which we get to accept through faith. Hence the greatest blessing is to be a child of God.

Blessing is always associated with God's power; it is either the demonstration of God's power or the appreciation of God's power. Baptism, benediction, sanctification, dedication and consecration are examples of blessing ceremonies that require the demonstration of God's power and must therefore be administered by God's representatives with God's power.

Thanksgiving, magnifying, glorifying, hallowing and exalting are ways we can show our appreciation of God's power; these are demonstrated by both the saved and the unsaved Christians.

Blessing something is real and effective only if it is administered by a true representative of God who is born again, because blessing involves grace from God, and only those saved by grace through faith have this grace. The priests, pastors, evangelists and ministers must all be true representatives of God before any blessing they offer will be effectively supported by God.

Benediction

In Numbers 6:24-26 God told Moses to inform Aaron and his children as priests to bless the children of Israel as follows: *"The Lord bless you and keep you; The Lord make His face shine upon you, And be gracious to you; The Lord lift up His countenance upon you, And give you peace."* Aaron and his sons were priests ordained by God, and therefore the representatives of God whose blessing would be real.

In Psalm 134:1-3 the blessing is *"Behold, bless the Lord, All you servants of the Lord, Who by night stand in the house of the Lord! Lift up your hands in the* sanctuary, And bless the Lord. The Lord who made heaven and earth, Bless you from Zion!"* The empowerment of this blessing is effective only if the officiating priest is born again and a true representative of God.

Other types of benediction are shown in 2 Corinthians 13:14, Ephesians 3:20-21, 1 Timothy 1:17, Hebrews 13:20-21, 1 Peter 5:10 and Jude 1:24-25.

Passages on people who are saved

Romans 4:7 tells us, *"Blessed are those whose lawless deeds are forgiven, and whose sins are covered."* Those whose iniquities are forgiven are those who are born again and therefore have the Spirit of God living in them.

Psalm 1:1-2 states *"Blessed is the man who walks not in the counsel of the ungodly, nor stands in the path of sinners, nor sits in the seat of the scornful; But his delight is in the law of the Lord, and in His law he meditates day and night."* This means the man who is godly and meditates on God's law day and night cannot commit sin and is blessed by God. This is a true Christian.

Psalm 2:12 states: *"Blessed are all those who put their trust in Him."* This refers to the Christians who are saved by grace because of their genuine faith in God.

In Psalm 41:1 we read, *"Blessed is he who considers the poor; The Lord will deliver him in time of trouble."* As God is merciful so are true Christians and therefore they support the poor for God's blessing.

We are reminded in Psalm 106:3, *"Blessed are they that keep judgment and he that doeth righteous at all times."* Since a true Christian is righteous at all times, he receives God's blessing.

Psalm 119:1 says, *"Blessed are those who keep justice, and he who does righteousness at all times!"* A true Christian is one who obeys God sincerely and therefore walks in the law of the Lord for blessing.

In Psalm 112:1 it is written, *"Blessed is the man who fears the Lord, who delights greatly in His commandments."* The man who fears God is one who obeys God by keeping God's commands. This man is a true Christian and is therefore blessed. This blessing is repeated in Psalm 128:1 as *"Blessed is everyone who fears the Lord, who walks in His ways."*

Psalm 119:2 reads *"Blessed are those who keep His testimonies, Who seek Him with the whole heart!"* Total surrender to God is imperative in order for one to be born again and to receive the Holy Ghost for God's blessing.

We're told in Revelation 1:3 that *"Blessed is he who reads and those who hear the words of this prophecy, and keep those things which are written in it; for the time is near."* In addition, Revelation 22:7 states, *"Behold, I am coming quickly! Blessed is he who keeps the words of the prophecy of this book."* These two verses emphasise that it is not just by hearing and reading the word of God that Christians receive a blessing, but it is by hearing, reading and keeping the word of God that one receives God's blessing. The emphasis is on the keeping of the word of God.

In Revelation 14:13 we read: *"Then I heard a voice from heaven saying to me, 'Write: "Blessed are the dead who die in the Lord from now on."' 'Yes,' says the Spirit, 'that they may rest from their labours, and their works follow them.'"* One who dies in the Lord is a Christian who dies in a sinless situation by being true to God to the end.

Regarding the resurrection, Revelation 20:6 states: *"Blessed and holy is he who has part in the first resurrection. Over such the second death has no power, but they shall be priests of God and of Christ, and shall reign with Him a thousand years."* Any Christian who dies in the Lord has part in the first resurrection and is blessed because he becomes a priest of God.

Conditions for blessings

The most important blessing is the grace of God which is meant for everybody, but the condition is that one has to accept it whole heartedly, with true faith in God. Hence Ephesians 2:8 affirms that *"by grace you have been saved through faith"*.

The next most important blessing is Holy Spirit baptism which is administered to those who are converted. Here conversion is the condition before the Holy Spirit is granted.

Every blessing has a condition attached to it, as can be seen from the passages quoted above, but the summary of all the conditions is that for one to be blessed by God one has to accept and obey God.

The Beatitudes (Matthew 5:3-11)

Beatitude means blessedness. The eight beatitudes summarise and describe all the qualities (and conditions) required of an ideal Christian and the blessings that go with them.

Verse 3: *"Blessed are the poor in spirit; for theirs is the kingdom of heaven."*

The poor in spirit are those who realise their natural helplessness and inadequacy in spirit and, with humility, surrender completely to God for spiritual richness. Such people are blessed to go to heaven.

Verse 4: *"Blessed are those who mourn; for they shall be comforted."* The people who mourn are those who genuinely repent of their sins and show genuine remorse not to sin again. These are the people who are genuinely converted and they are rewarded by the Holy Spirit, the comforter.

Verse 5: *"Blessed are the meek; for they shall inherit the earth."* Those who are gentle, humble, mild and submissive shall inherit the earth.

Verse 6: *"Blessed are those who hunger and thirst for righteousness, for they shall be filled."* These are the people who genuinely desire to do what is right, and to achieve this is to genuinely desire to serve God. He grants them the Holy Spirit so they are filled with righteousness.

Verse 7: *"Blessed are the merciful; for they shall obtain mercy."* Those who show kindness, compassion, sympathy, empathy, leniency and forgiveness are merciful and therefore obtain mercy from God.

Verse 8: *"Blessed are the pure in heart; for they shall see God."* The people who are holy and righteous and therefore sinless, qualify to see God.

Verse 9: *"Blessed are the peacemakers; for they shall be called the sons of God."* For one to be a peacemaker the person's mind should be at peace, and to be at peace is to have the body, spirit and soul together, which means God dwells in the person. Such a person also brings peace to others and is indeed a child of God.

Verse 10: *"Blessed are those who are persecuted for righteousness' sake, for theirs is the kingdom of heaven."* The righteous are those who have the Holy Spirit living in them and should expect persecution for their righteousness because they are not of the world. Such people are blessed because they qualify to go to the kingdom of heaven.

These eight attributes are the eight conditions to be fulfilled by a perfect Christian in order to obtain all the blessings from God.

Conclusion

There are two types of blessing – a favour from God to man which is the grace and power from God, and then a reciprocal acknowledgement and appreciation of the grace of God from man. The greatest blessing God gave to man is the forgiveness of his sins, and the greatest blessing man gives God is man's acceptance of the blessing through appreciation. Hence we are saved by the grace of God through our genuine belief in God. God is therefore the source of any blessing and blessing is genuinely and effectively administered only by true believers of God.

The blessing from God and reciprocal blessing from a Christian to God is vividly shown in Psalm 103:1-5 where God restores a Christian's soul as a blessing and the Christian uses his soul and his whole being to thank God as a blessing. Because God has blessed him with a soul, the following blessings flow: forgiveness of iniquities, healing of diseases, redemption from destruction, crowning with lovingkindness and tender mercies.

CHAPTER 32

MY EXPERIENCE WITH EVIL SPIRITS

My first encounter with evil spirits was in May 1978 when I was a deputy principal at Nkawie Toase Secondary School in Ghana.

Barely five minutes after lying down on my bed after my normal mid-night prayer in my semi-detached bungalow on the school campus, I saw a short man about one metre high with an abnormally big head suddenly appear from nowhere at the entrance of my locked chamber door.

The doorway was directly opposite my altar (the holy place in my room where I always prayed) and about six metres away. The evil spirit walked straight towards the altar and it was about one metre away from the altar when it stopped briefly, shook its head and turned 180 degrees and went back to the doorway and vanished.

Exactly two weeks after my encounter with the evil spirit, on a Sunday at about 7.30am when my family and I were about to leave the house to go to church, we saw objects of different kinds including stones, cobs and pieces of burned wood being thrown onto the rooftop of the house by invisible beings. A crowd of people gathered around the house was equally bewildered about the incredible situation.

I left the house with my family to attend a church service about 20km away. On our return from church four hours later, we saw the crowd had dispersed but the rooftop and the ground were littered with the materials the evil spirits had thrown about.

My family and another family lived in the two semi-detached bungalows which had a common roof, and while we were away attending church service, the history teacher, who was in the other house consulted a juju man who happened to deal with dwarfs to find out what had happened in our houses.

The dwarfs told their master, the juju man, that they were not causing the trouble but suspected some dwarfs who belonged to another juju man staying about 40km away from their place. Their master then sent the dwarfs to contact the other dwarfs to find out what had happened at our place of residence.

Before long the dwarfs returned to their master to confirm that the other dwarfs had indeed caused the trouble at our place. According to them somebody had paid money to their master asking him to kill the person who had deprived that person of his daily bread.

When the history teacher told me about the information he received from the juju man it reminded me of my encounter with a dwarf entering my bedroom two weeks earlier. This confirmed that the dwarf I saw after my mid-night prayer had intended to kill me. How can a dwarf kill a child of God like me who has the Spirit of God living in him?

During that time I was acting as principal since the principal had taken a long leave of absence after the death of his uncle who was a renowned chief of his home town and the Ashanti region as a whole.

While I was Acting Principal a business economics teacher in the school was not attending classes regularly so the students in his classes reported him to me. I called him on three occasions to warn him about his absenteeism but he continued to attend classes irregularly so I had no option but to report him to the Regional Director of Education and he was eventually dismissed. I also dismissed my laboratory assistant for his laziness, incompetence and irregular class attendance. I thus suspected that one of the two or both of them might have gone to see the juju man to get his dwarfs to kill me.

How can any evil spirit kill a true Christian like me who has the Holy Spirit in him and is therefore a child of God? This is a lesson to both real Christians and nominal Christians that whoever does not have the Holy Spirit in him can be killed by evil spirits at any time. The Bible states in Ecclesiastes 7:17, *"Why should you die before your time?"* because a person who is not a child of God with the Holy Spirit in him can die before the time God intended for his death.

Psalm 90:10 states *"The days of our lives are seventy years; And if by reason of strength they are eighty years, Yet their boast is only labour and sorrow; For it is soon cut off, and we fly away."* Whoever is born into the world has a set lifespan given by God. Whoever is born again and becomes a child of God has a lifespan controlled by God and dies according to the lifespan and the will of

God and goes back to God. Whoever is not born again of God is controlled by Satan and therefore may die at any time.

My second encounter with evil spirits

My second encounter with evil spirits occurred in South Africa in 1992 when I was Principal of the Ikhala Technical College and also the Head of Science Department of Sterkspruit Senior Secondary School.

During one of the matric exams in 1992 a student collapsed while writing a paper, so she was brought to my office. I prayed for her and when she regained consciousness I asked what had happened to her. She told me that in the previous year she could not write the matric exam because whenever she sat down to write a paper she would fall down. Her parents took her to various places to see spiritualists, witchdoctors, jujumen and sangomas, so she thought everything was all right and that she could write the following year's matric exam, but lo and behold she fell down during the first paper.

I assured her that God would deliver her from her problems. I told her that we were going to fast with her for not less than forty days, which she agreed to. Indeed she fasted for forty days but my wife and I fasted for forty-seven and fifty-four days respectively.

When we started fasting we went to see the parents and they gladly agreed. However, two days later her elder brother, who was, a policeman, told the parents that his supervisor was a developed ZCC pastor so he could deliver his sister. We allowed her to go home and continue with the fasting but warned her never to eat or drink anything the ZCC pastor gave her.

Three days later three hefty ZCC members went to her house to pray for her and offered to give her a drink which they called *"tea"*. She was reluctant and refused to take it because we had warned her, but the three hefty ZCC men forced her to take the tea.

The following morning the girl came to my office with the intention of telling me that she had been forced to take tea by the ZCC men. However, as soon as she stepped through my office door she fell down and the evil spirit started manifesting. The evil spirit said he was hungry and wanted food to eat. I told him that the girl was fasting for forty days so no food would be given to her. The evil spirit then asked that the girl's sister-in-law, the wife of the policeman, and a teacher in the school be called for him. When she came, the evil spirit told her that he was hungry and wanted food to eat. I told the evil spirit that she would not give him any food to eat.

Then the evil spirit told her that her husband, the policeman, was not a Christian. The spirit also told her that they, the evil spirits, were in the tea that her husband and the ZCC pastor forced the girl to drink, and so they came back into the girl. Before that they had been expelled from her due to my prayers and fasting. The evil spirit told the woman that one of the evil spirits entered her husband for him to speak disrespectfully to me, because their intention was to make me angry so that I would leave the girl and stop praying and fasting for her.

The policeman was a young man who usually had much respect for me, so I had been surprised that during that time he spoke to me disrespectfully, but I ignored it and was not angry as the evil spirits had expected.

The next manifestation of the evil spirit was during our Christian fellowship meeting in my residence. Again the girl fell down and the evil spirit started talking. The evil spirit said an angel of God was at the throne of God commanding them to leave the girl's body; they had been stubborn and resisting but they would have to leave. So I asked the evil spirit what an angel looked like. The evil spirit smiled and responded as follows: *"Mr Asibey, don't you see an angel behind you? Don't you see an angel by the door opposite to you? There are angels here."* Then the evil spirit pointed at some of the fellowship members and said. *"This girl fornicates. The other girl takes alcohol. They are not supposed to be here in the fellowship."* The evil spirit said my residence was surrounded by fire so the evil spirits could not enter unless they had occupied the bodies of the sinners before they entered my residence.

Some weeks later when the girl was with her peers in a classroom she fell down and the evil spirit started manifesting again.

I was in my office when the girl fell down and another girl came to tell me what had happened. When I went to the classroom the other learners told me that the evil spirit was saying that Mr Asibey was coming to burn him. When I got there the girl was still lying down on the floor so I asked the evil spirit how many of them were in her body. The evil spirit laughed and quickly responded saying that there had been thirty, but twenty-nine of them had left the body and only he remained. He said that he was Beelzebub, the chief demon, but that he would soon be leaving the girl's body. I asked the evil spirit more questions but he kept quiet for some time and would not say anything, then later on he said *"Mr Asibey, the more I talk to you the more I lose my power and that is why at times I keep quiet."*

Finally, about two weeks later, when the girl was leaning against a couch in our sitting room the evil spirit started manifesting again, saying, *"Mr Asibey we are not in your sitting room here but on the rooftop of the Cash and Carry building next to your residence. We are speaking through her from here. We are from Durban."* (Durban is 1 000km away from Sterkspruit.)

"We have been banished from our original place in Durban because we could not fulfil the mission for which we were sent, namely to kill the girl. We are leaving her now because she has been saved through you, but warn her that if she goes against the teachings you have given her we shall come back to destroy her."

After this utterance from the evil spirits the girl regained consciousness. I told her of the warning from the evil spirits and advised her to continue with the teachings I had given her. As I write this book now, twenty-eight years after the warning from the evil spirits to the girl, they have never come back to disturb her. That girl is now a successful woman with a high post in the Department of Health in South Africa.

Conclusion

These reports of my personal experiences with evil spirits should be enough to warn you as a true Christian or a nominal Christian or a non-Christian that evil spirits are real. As is written in 1 John 5:18 *"We know that whoever is born of God does not sin; but he who has been born of God keeps himself, and the wicked one does not touch him."* Satan is the devil and therefore all evil spirits come under him and they are all wicked.

Since only about ten percent of churchgoers are true Christians and therefore do not commit any sin, they are the only people that Satan cannot touch to destroy. Since about ninety percent of churchgoers are nominal Christians and therefore commit at least one sin wilfully, evil spirits can touch and destroy them. Are you a sinless Christian or a sinful Christian? God knows, you know and Satan knows.

God bless you for your sinlessness; heaven is your eternal home.

CHAPTER 33

MY CHURCH

My church is called Thearchical Domain. "Theo" means God, "Archin'" means father, and "Domain" means kingdom. Thearchical Domain is therefore God the Father's kingdom. It is the kingdom which Jesus Christ mentioned in the Lord's Prayer – "Thy kingdom come". It is this kingdom which came in 1990.

The founder of the church is Thearc Daniel Kingsley Arthur who saw God on 23 December 1952. His spirit had already been taken to see soul heaven (sixth heaven) just as the spirit of Paul was taken to see heaven paradise (fourth heaven). Thearchical Domain Church was founded in 1956. According to Thearc Daniel, any church founded on Jesus Christ has to undergo three phases of spiritual development within thirty years. When it was established in 1956, the church was called Mystic Brotherhood. For the second phase it was called Mystery School, and for the third and final phase it is called Thearchical Domain. That has been its name since 1990.

In his book "Mystical Experience", Thearc Daniel describes how he saw God: "I steadfastly took the laws of God into strict adherence by practising justice, avoiding abominations and ostracisms throughout my daily life. I pursued the art of strict holiness, having no sexual affairs for many years.

"With fortitude and fervent meditations every day, it was in the mid-night of December 23, 1952, when I fell into a deep trance. I saw a powerful light piercing through the ceiling, directly to my bed where I was lying. I saw the sky very calm and clear as crystal. Immediately, the clouds began to gather up in big sizes, and I saw a very bright figure in the shape of a person floating therein. The scene came into a clearer view and behold, there stood a man, very beautiful and lovely to look upon, with a body which gives light brighter than any electric light. I was told that he was Jehovah – the omnipotent God.

"He was covered with the rainbow, in an oval shape, standing in a tranquil majesty of his Lordly form, in alertness as an expert soldier. His eyes were shining like a flaming fire, and he was dressed in a purple toga with a green short cassock underneath. A powerful yellowish light streamed from him in a terrific manner like a whirlwind towards me. As the light was shining on me, my spirit stood aside, leaving the body motionless. My spirit was looking at my body and God in reverential fear. Then God pointed at me with a forefinger, with such a power piercing through my body as if it were an arrow thrust through my body. The power from the finger flashed and made my spirit spring to another position in amazement. Then God uttered in a commanding voice, 'You are a saint' with such a thunderous volume that my spirit sprang farther apart for the third time.

"Immediately afterwards some inscriptions appeared, similar to two triangles one opposite the other. I was asked to explain the meaning, but I could not because it was beyond my comprehension. Then God, squeezing his eyebrows exclaimed 'Death!' flashing his hand from the east to the west with power like lightning. After the explanation, the clouds covered up and my spirit sprang from the three points and entered my body. I woke up very weak and trembling but very refreshed and satisfied. Thus ended my determination to see God and that has been what I willed to be and have become immortal."

Thearchical Domain Church is also called Soul Church because the doctrine is called psychism. "Psyche" is soul. The founder describes the church as: The end of Christian development; the university church of God; the peak of holiness and righteousness; the seventh and final grade of the work of the Holy Spirit; the congregation of saints.

Thearc Daniel describes the soul doctrine as: The perfect doctrine of God; the path of the second coming of Jesus Christ; the only means of the acquisition and maintenance of the Holy Spirit; the last trumpet of the word of God; the esoteric art of God given to man through the Holy Spirit; the new philosophy of the highest development in Christ; and, through the science of the created and uncreated elements, the climax of the Christian doctrine.

According to the founder of the church, psychism is the last Christian doctrine of Christendom. It is the seventh and the last spirit of the seven spirits of God, establishing the last church – Thearchical Domain.

In soul doctrine both the Old Testament and the New Testament – the Father's worship and the Son's worship – are kept so that both the body and the spirit are holy.

In Leviticus 11:44-46 God says He is holy and so we must be holy, and for one to be holy one should keep the laws of the beast etc. By keeping these laws one's body becomes holy.

In John 3:3 Jesus says one must be born of water and of the spirit to enter into the kingdom of God. When one is born of the spirit that means one is granted the Holy Spirit. That means that, for the Son's worship, the New Testament, one must receive the Holy Spirit in order for one's spirit to be holy.

When the body is holy and the spirit is also holy this is perfect holiness. This is where a member of the church practices justice and avoids abominations and ostracism. Justice is a just conduct. It is righteousness, uprightness, goodness and honesty exhibited by Christians because of the Holy Spirit in them. Abominations are serious sins, fornication/adultery, alcohol and smoking, which are incompatible with the Holy Spirit, and all Christians should avoid them because the body is the temple of God. Ostracisms are unclean things which some Christians avoid for the body to be holy. Christians who avoid ostracisms by avoiding pollution of the body, including the law of the beast as stated in Leviticus 11, are the first-class saints who go to soul heaven right away after death.

Membership

For a person to become a full member of the church, the person meets the elders of the church who will teach the person the principles of the church. The person is given a probationary period of three months and fasts using special psalms for three days. The person is then baptised with the impartation of the Holy Spirit.

The sacredness of the church

Because God is holy, the place of worship is kept holy. Hence the following rules are observed. Footwear is left outside the church. A woman in her menstrual cycle should not enter the church. A dead body is never allowed to enter the church. Any indecently dressed person, including women wearing trousers, is not allowed to enter the church. Women should put on a veil to cover their heads at church service.

Fasting

It is imperative that members fast. We fast twice a week, on Wednesday and Saturday. Every third week we fast for three days from Wednesday to Friday and give alms on the Friday. Hence in a year of 365 days, we fast for at least 121 days, because at times we fast for a week or more for special situations. For normal fasting we do not eat any food or drink any liquid from 6am to 6pm. Members on medication or who are very old are granted a moderate fasting. During congregational fasting we often use some of the following psalms: 51, 65, 70, 23, 27, 91, 46 and 130. We usually pray for the individual, the church, the country and the world at large. The longest fast I ever did was daily from 6am to 6pm without food or liquid for four years five months from 22 September 1995 to 22 February 2000. My wife fasted for four years within that period. All this was done for spiritual upliftment.

The responsibility of the members is to pay monthly membership dues. Members are encouraged to also pay their quarterly and thanksgiving offerings, and voluntary contributions for specific projects are welcomed.

Order of service on Sundays

The service is conducted by a preacher ordained by God. It is a solemn assembly controlled by the preacher. The songs that are sung come from the chanting of psalms from the Psalter, the singing of hymns from the Methodist hymn book and the singing of spiritual songs. As it's written in Colossians 3:16 *"Let the word of Christ dwell in you richly in all wisdom, teaching and admonishing one another in psalms and hymns and spiritual songs, singing with grace in your hearts to the Lord."*

The preacher makes a general announcement including emphasising some salient points for spiritual development. For the sermon, the preacher often reads a chapter of the Bible and explains it. Four prayers are offered, each while the congregation is kneeling down. Money offerings are collected during the service. The service takes an average of two and a half hours.

All the preachers of the Thearchical Domain Church emphasise the following:

- The only way to heaven is sinlessness.

- The only way to attain sinlessness is through repentance, conversion and baptism to obtain the Holy Ghost.

- Maintaining the Holy Ghost to the end leads to heaven.

- Mankind's only enemy is Satan.

- Mankind's only problem is sin.

Church attendance

Members are required to attend service every Sunday — except the women in their menstrual cycle. Any member who is absent for three consecutive Sundays or more reports to the body of preachers before resuming attendance of church service on his/her return.

If a member absents himself/herself for three consecutive months, the committee sends a delegation to visit the member to find out what the problem is.

Suspension and dismissal

If it is proved beyond doubt that a member has committed fornication, smoked or taken alcohol or shown insubordination or anything contrary to the principles of the Church, the member is suspended by the committee of elders. Counselling and guidance is given to the member, and if he adheres to that and genuinely repents he is given another chance, but if not, then the member is not recalled.

Implications of suspension and dismissal

If a member is suspended or dismissed they cease to be a member of the Church. They may or may not be recalled. The sin committed separates the member from God and so the Spirit of God has been withdrawn from them. If the member dies while they're suspended they cannot go to heaven. If a member dies while suspended the Church cannot bury them and Satan has access to them.

Initiating recall

In order for a member to be recalled there needs to be acceptance of guilt, repentance, fervent prayer and fasting for forgiveness as well as a desire for recall. The member must then write to the elders telling them he/she is sorry for the wrongdoing, apologising for the wrongdoing, requesting psalms for fasting and making a vow not to do anything wrong again.

Restoration

God directs how a member is restored, but it includes them fasting for a set number of days and being baptised again for the restoration of the soul.

Marriage

The Church is very serious about marriage. When a person is born again, the next important thing to do is to marry. The Church encourages marriage among the members. Should a member fall in love with somebody who is not a member of Thearchical Domain Church, that person should become a member of the Church and be born again before the Church approves of the marriage. We have on record some members of the Church who got married outside the Church and went to other churches with their spouses, backslid and lost the Holy Spirit, and we want to avoid that.

Support for the needy

Members who are in need are encouraged to see the committee of elders to discuss their problems. Students are supported to further their education, and the aged, the sick and the widowed are supported financially and otherwise where necessary.

Funerals and benefits

The Church reserves the right to bury her dead within a week or two provided the deceased was an active member and not more than three months in arrears in respect of membership dues. If a member is in good standing, the Church will take care of the ablution of the remains, the provision of shrouds and coffin and the ceremony of the actual interment. Free donations from members are encouraged to defray any extra funeral expenses.

The Church donates a specific amount to a bereaved member who loses a spouse who is also a member. If the spouse is not a member, half of the stipulated amount is donated.

The corpse is never taken into the church because it is a holy place and must never be polluted. No food or drink is served there and nobody is allowed to eat or drink at the funeral because wherever there is a corpse the place is polluted. Members are not to eat or drink at any funeral they attend. There is also no washing of hands in a bowl of water provided at some funerals. Members only eat or drink after funerals and after washing.

Eating habits

Members avoid eating outside their homes (for example in restaurants) as much as possible, because of pollution. Members avoid eating or drinking from the same bowl with others. Members keep the laws of the beast where some meat, fish and fowls — especially pork and all the related products — are not eaten, according to the laws stated in Leviticus 11.

Dressing

The Church encourages moderate and decent dressing because the body is the temple of God. Women are not allowed to wear trousers (Deuteronomy 22:5) in the church or anywhere else because wherever a born again Christian is, God is still in the person. Simple earrings and decent dressing are encouraged. No make-up like lipstick, nail polish, eye shadow or mascara is permitted.

Conclusion

The only aim of the Church is to see to it that each member is born again. To attain this, the preachers are all saints sent by God to preach for the members to repent, be converted and be baptised and, by impartation, to receive the Holy Ghost. Since the church was founded by Thearc Daniel who saw God and whose spirit was also taken to the soul heaven, and who was guided by God to establish this Soul Church, the principles of Thearchical Domain Church remain the same. Should all churches come together to form one church, this church will still remain the same unless all churches come to join this church.

Do your best to find a way to visit the Soul Church, founded by Jesus Christ through the person of Thearc Daniel Arthur after he saw God in 1952.

Saint Alex Osei Nketia-Asibey BSc., PGCE, Bed. Med.

Christian Psychist Ordained as a saint by Thearc Daniel Kingsley Arthur, the man who saw God on 23 December 1952 and also saw soul heaven, heaven paradise and hell.

ABOUT THE AUTHOR

Saint Alex Asibey has been a Christian since childhood. He was very active in Christian movements from high school up to university. After he graduated with a Bachelor of Science in Physics and Mathematics in 1966, he took up teaching as a profession and became the Head of the Science Department in every high school where he taught. He was an Education Specialist (School-Based) from September 1966 to November 2005.

Saint Alex Asibey was ordained a Saint Psychist Preacher in 1970 by the leader of his church, Thearc Daniel Arthur, who saw God in December 1952. The leader's spirit was also taken to see hell, heaven paradise (fourth heaven) and the psychic realm (soul heaven or sixth heaven). Since his ordination as a preacher, Saint Alex has been preaching in his church. He has also been baptising by impartation of spirit baptism.

Saint Alex Asibey used his position as a Physics and Mathematics teacher to do evangelism in all the schools he taught, by opening a Students' Christian Movement. He taught them how to become Christians and the benefits of being Christians. He also taught them the necessity of fasting to support their prayers and spiritual growth.

Schools where he taught

Saint Alex Asibey has taught in a number of schools, in and outside of South Africa. He has also assumed the roles of Deputy Principal and Principal in a number of these schools.

Ghana (1966-1978): Suhum Secondary Technical School and Nkawie Toase Secondary School.

Lesotho (1978-1982): Peka High School and Thabeng High School.

Swaziland (1982 -1984): Ngwane High School.

South Africa (1984-2005): Sterkspruit Senior Secondary School and Ikhala TVET College.

He has led a life of fasting, and his first three days of dry fasting were done a few days after his matriculation. Since the time he entered university, he has been fasting a minimum of two days a week, on every Wednesday and Saturday. In 1992 he fasted for 54 days and, by the power of the Almighty

God, cast out thirty demons which possessed one of his students. The last demon to leave her body made an utterance and claimed to be Beelzebub, the chief demon. Saint Alex's longest fast was a daily normal fasting of not taking food or liquid from 6am to 6pm from 22 September 1995 to 22 February 2000, during which he prayed to God that he would be endowed with power and the gifts of the Holy Spirit to do the greater work of God. He stopped fasting when Doctor Bogaden of Unitas Hospital in Pretoria, South Africa, conducted a gastroscopy examination and diagnosed that he had a gastric ulcer. Saint Alex then prayed to God and was healed miraculously by God.

Qualifications

Bachelor of Science

Postgraduate Certificate in Education

Bachelor of Education

Master's in Education

A branch of Saint Alex Asibey's Church, Thearchical Domain, was established in Centurion, Pretoria, South Africa, in 2000.

www.ingramcontent.com/pod-product-compliance
Lightning Source LLC
Chambersburg PA
CBHW061431040426
42450CB00007B/1004